GRAPHIC WITNESS

FOUR WORDLESS GRAPHIC NOVELS

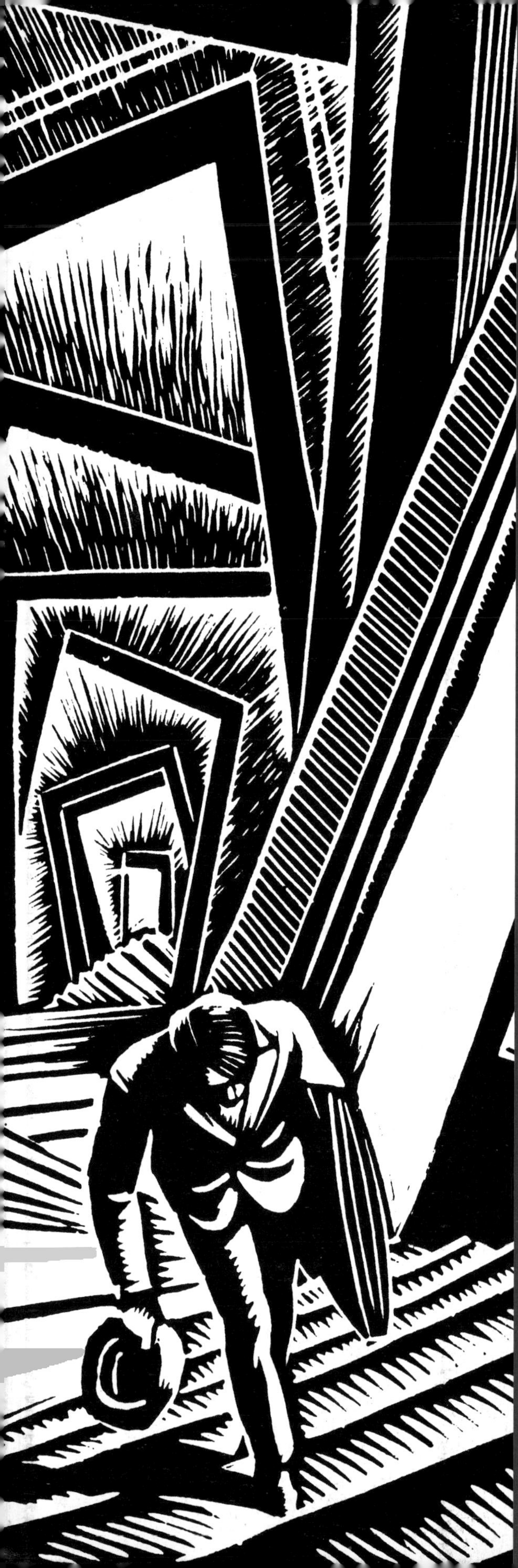

GRAPHIC WITNESS

Four Wordless Graphic Novels

FRANS MASEREEL
LYND WARD
GIACOMO PATRI
LAURENCE HYDE

Selected and Introduced by
GEORGE A. WALKER

FIREFLY BOOKS

A FIREFLY BOOK

Published by Firefly Books Ltd. 2007

First printing

Publisher Cataloging-in-Publication Data (U.S.)
Graphic witness / four wordless graphic novels by Frans Masereel, Lynd Ward, Giacomo
Patri and Laurence Hyde ; introduction by George A. Walker.
[   ] p. : ill. ; cm.
Includes bibliographical references and index.
Summary: An anthology of four wordless novels by artists Frans Masereel, Lynd Ward,
Giacomo Patri and Laurence Hyde, and a look at how these artists used their work as a
form of social commentary. The influence of this art form on modern filmmaking and the
graphic novel is also examined.
ISBN-13: 978-1-55407-270-5 (pbk.)
ISBN-10: 1-55407-270-0 (pbk.)
1. Graphic novels. I. Walker, George A. (George Alexander), 1960-. II. Title.
741.59 dc22   NE1096.G737 2007

Library and Archives Canada Cataloguing in Publication
Graphic witness : four wordless graphic novels by Frans Masereel, Lynd Ward,
Giacomo Patri and Laurence Hyde / selected and introduced by
George A. Walker.
Includes bibliographical references and index.
ISBN-13: 978-1-55407-270-5
ISBN-10: 1-55407-270-0
1. Graphic novels. I. Walker, George A. (George Alexander), 1960-
NE1096.G73 2007   741.5'9   C2007-900280-3

Published in the United States by
Firefly Books (U.S.) Inc.
P.O. Box 1338, Ellicott Station
Buffalo, New York 14205

Published in Canada by
Firefly Books Ltd.
66 Leek Crescent
Richmond Hill, Ontario L4B 1H1

Cover and interior design: Kathe Gray/electric pear
Printed in China

*The publisher gratefully acknowledges the financial support for
our publishing program by the Government of Canada through
the Book Publishing Industry Development Program.*

To my wife Michelle
for all her support and encouragement
and to my sons Dylan and Nicholas
who will see in these picture novels
that history does indeed repeat itself.

PREFACE

I magine the advantage of writing a book that can be read anywhere in the world without translation. Free of the confines of words, books written in the universal language of pictures are understandable anywhere in the global village. A drawing of a stick figure needs no translation. Pictorial narratives are not new; the earliest known cave paintings told tales of hunting, the Egyptians used sequential images and all written languages evolved from pictures, our universal system of expression and communication.

My fascination with the wordless novel began in the 1980s, after attending an exhibition at the Art Gallery of Ontario featuring the work of Frans Masereel, who is regarded as the first master of the wordless novel. After the exhibition I began an obsessive pursuit to find books illustrated with woodcuts, wood engravings and linocuts, and to learn everything I could about fine art printmaking and the art of wood engraving.

Living in a rough part of the city, being desperately poor and struggling to balance college expenses with low-paying part-time work, I often felt like a character in a Masereel novel. The building that I lived in housed a vegetable soup of characters, ranging from prostitutes to con men. I once had to disarm a kid, not much older than 10, who pulled a knife on me and demanded my bike. At the time words didn't seem able to communicate my feelings—pictures seemed more poignant and accessible to illustrate this world. It was exhilarating to plaster my woodcuts in the neighborhood, criticizing the landlord and poking fun at the politics and injustices of the day, and today I can identify with Masereel's words: "Since the time of my youth, I have protested against the society in which I am living. The social injustice seemed odious to me, and I believe that this early rebellion became the source of many of my works."

Wordless novels have often treated controversial themes and been associated with protest movements. The early part of the 20th century saw the technological advances of the industrial revolution, yet life was becoming increasingly difficult for the average worker. A literate and socially conscious middle class was growing, with expectations of a better life for everyone. These expectations were interrupted by a war, an economic depression, another war, the cold war and the looming threat of nuclear annihilation.

The works in this book, products of these difficult times, were created in Europe, the United States and Canada between 1918 and 1951. The political and social issues they address are specific to their times, but the broader issues are, sadly, still relevant to our contemporary eyes.

Masereel created his first wordless novel, *The Passion of a Man,* in 1918, using only 25 woodcuts. That little book influenced three generations of artists, writers, musicians, animators and filmmakers, yet his work has remained largely unknown in North America. Only now, at the beginning of the 21st century, is Masereel being rediscovered as one of the most important graphic artists of the 20th century and the grandfather of the modern graphic novel.

This book includes the work of four of the greatest wordless novelists who used relief-printmaking techniques: Frans Masereel, Lynd Ward, Giacomo Patri and Laurence Hyde. These men were artistic and literary masters of the form.

There are, of course, other artists of this period who also expressed their ideas in wordless books. The horrors of war and social injustice seem particularly fit subjects for this art. In 1957, Si Lewen, who was influenced by Frans Masereel and George Grosz, created an antiwar visual narrative, *The Parade,* a story in 55 drawings that showed the ugly realities of battle and death that lay behind the pomp and ceremony of military parades. In his introduction to the book, Albert Einstein wrote about the power of art to "counteract the tendencies towards war," and said that nothing "can equal the psychological effect of real art—neither factual descriptions nor intellectual discussions." This statement rings true for all the wordless novels that appear in the pages that follow.

As well as a medium of social protest, the wordless novel has also had an important influence on popular culture. There is an undeniable relationship between the making of film storyboards and the sequential art of the wordless novel. Frans Masereel was interested in cinema, and in 1932 Berthold Bartosch turned Masereel's wordless novel *The Idea* into an animated film. Masereel had intended to work on the film with Bartosch, but the task was too time-consuming and Masereel left Bartosch with creative license to interpret his book. The result is a true art film. Bartosch translated the characters into his own painterly style of layers and cutouts, giving a nod to Masereel and his woodcuts and drawings. We are lucky to be able to see any of Bartosch's work today—and particularly a film made from a book by Masereel—since the Nazis tried to destroy everything by both artists.

In many respects the wordless novel is the simplest form of reading. It has an undeniable relation to the modern comic strip, but wordless novels are not books for children—or "comic books," as we might define them today. They are sequential art for adults; "picture novels," "wordless novels" or "graphic narratives" are how their creators defined them. They have inspired a generation of artists and are important works illustrating how social change and political strife are as much an inspiration to the artist as they are a provocateur to oppression.

It is important to note that artists working in the comic book style were aware of the power of the wordless novels of Masereel and others. Milt Gross' *He Done Her Wrong* (1930) is a wordless story about love and misunderstanding. It is actually a parody of the wordless novel that was being made famous in the United States by Lynd Ward. Myron Waldman's *Eve*, another comic wordless story in pictures, was published in 1943. Waldman is famous for his work at the Max Fleischer animation studios, where he worked on cartoons such as *Betty Boop, Superman* and *Popeye*. His book, too, is in the comic book style of sequential images, with drawings splashed across the page spreads in a playful manner.

An earlier example is *Mitsou,* created by the French painter Balthus and published in 1921, which tells the story of the author's cat, Mitsou. Balthus' pen-and-ink drawings follow a style not unlike Masereel's earlier wood engravings. Balthus made the images when he was only 13, lending charm and naïveté to the work. It featured an introduction by Rainer Maria Rilke, one of the greatest poets of the 20th century—a highly respectable endorsement for a story without words.

Much later, Will Eisner's *A Contract with God* (1978) and Art Spiegelman's Pulitzer Prize–winning *Maus* (1986) were published to critical and popular acclaim. Although neither is a comic book—and the themes of both are closer to tragedy than comedy—Eisner and Spiegelman are considered by some to be comic book artists. Eisner's *Storytelling and Visual Narrative* (1996) is in effect a how-to guide on the use of the graphic narrative, as is Scott McCloud's *Understanding Comics* (1993).

Works by Eisner and his contemporaries led the way for the emergence of the modern graphic novel that incorporates both text and image. Writers like Neil Gaiman, Alan Moore, Joe Sacco, Harvey Pekar, Frank Miller and Chris Ware are just a few of the stars of this evolving art form. In 2001, controversy surrounded the Guardian First Book Award presented to Chris Ware for his graphic novel *Jimmy Corrigan, The Smartest Kid on Earth.* The jury wasn't unanimous that the award should go to a graphic novel, and there is much debate about the graphic novel abandoning its comic book roots for a more adult audience. The popularity of the graphic novel demonstrates that it has come into the mainstream for readers young and old alike.

Another popular form of the modern graphic novel is seen in the Manga books from Japan, which have evolved from the Japanese woodcut tradition. The great Japanese artist Hokusai (1760–1849) coined the term Manga, which roughly translates as *whimsical pictures.* His works were not graphic narratives, but stylized woodcuts depicting Japanese culture.

Modern Manga novels are illustrated with exaggerated characters drawn with large eyes and cartoon features. They gradually began to address adult topics in their stories, and their popularity gained accordingly. Like comic books in the West, Manga began as serial stories in magazines. In the 1950s the artist Yoshihiro Tatsumi started a new type of adult graphic novel called "Gekiga," or "dramatic picture books." These books were not for children; the artwork was more refined and detailed, and dealt with more serious subject matters than the Manga artwork. The "Gekiga" has evolved into the *Nouvelle Manga,* an artistic movement combining French, Belgian and Japanese comic book styles. It is fitting that the adult graphic novel tradition begun by the Belgian Frans Masereel has circled the globe and arrived back where it started, albeit changed by its long journey.

Even though the wordless novels of Frans Masereel and his followers have become rare collectors' items, they have found new life in the hands of antiquarian booksellers. Sought after by graphic novel collectors for their influence on comic book artists and coveted by print collectors, these books are enjoying a new attraction for younger generations.

As a woodcut artist, I've always been attracted to black-and-white art. I think it has something to do with the rich contrasts. I love a deep rich black that you can stare into, forever. The effect is like our colorful world torn down to its base so that we can read the underlying message. The truth is always easier to take in black and white. Typography is always more legible in black and white, so why would we be surprised to find the readability of artworks enhanced by those contrasts? Remove the grays and hues, reduce the image to lines and solid blacks, and open up the whites. You have a thing of beauty and simplicity.

Another way to understand our attraction to black and white is through the science of how we see. The human eye consists of rods and cones that process the reflected light of our world. These signals are then translated into color and form for processing by our brain. The rods, which are sensitive only to black and white, are the first components activated in a baby's eyes. That's why infants readily respond to high-contrast black-and-white images. We are hardwired to appreciate black-and-white artwork.

Let's not resist its temptation. I know I can't.

— *George A. Walker*

INTRODUCTION

The wordless novels reproduced in this book were created using relief-printing techniques. Relief printing is the oldest form of printmaking, tracing its beginnings back to eighth century China, where it was used to print devotional charms and later to decorate fabric. The first woodcuts appeared in Europe in the 15th century, and their popularity spread rapidly. Albrecht Dürer (1471–1528) was one of several artists who made a handsome sum selling impressions from their woodcuts.

The basic idea of relief printing is to create an image that can be transferred to paper from the raised surface of the block. First the artist draws or transfers the image onto a block prepared for printing, and then he or she cuts away those areas that are not to be printed. The raised portion of the block is rolled with ink and a piece of paper laid over it. Next the artist takes an impression from the surface by burnishing the paper with the back of a spoon. (Alternatively, and for faster printing, the block can be run through a printing press.) The image produced on the paper mirrors that on the block. Blocks for relief printing can be made from wood, linoleum, metal or other materials, such as plastic or rubber. This is the simplest form of printmaking and therefore the most accessible for a poor artist with few resources. It is often referred to as the art of the white line because it is a subtractive process that works from black to white. To make a black line the artist must carve two white lines, since the wood must be removed from both sides of the line that is to print.

Woodcutting and wood engraving involve different methods of printmaking. Wood engravings are cut on the end grain of the wood, while woodcuts are cut on the plank. The difference is seen in the details that can be achieved with wood engraving. By the 1850s, craftsmen could engrave photographs on the end grain of the wood. Blocks for wood engraving can take hours to prepare and are cut with the tiny tools of the silversmith. If that job isn't sufficiently intensive, imagine using this method to tell a story in pictures. An artist needs to cut many blocks to tell even the simplest of stories. It is also important to remember that a slip of the tool across the surface of the block will render an image useless for printing. Erasing a line is not an option once it is incised in the surface. It takes a careful and sure hand to create a block ready for printing. When you see the images in this book, look for those stray white lines that appear like scratches across the black areas. These are the marks where the tool has slipped.

The artists who made the four books reproduced in this volume chose relief-printing techniques (wood engravings and linoleum cuts) to tell their stories. For them, it was a perfect medium — accessible, easy to reproduce, enduring and with a voice of its own — to promote the cause of social justice. For the public, prints are less expensive and more easily obtainable than original paintings. The medium has also been cherished by publishers, since the printmaker is able to provide the blocks ready for printing, eliminating the cost of making plates.

Although passionate advocates of change, these wordless novels are not primarily political art. Frans Masereel, the inventor of the wordless novel, said that "politics is a matter of factions — in Italian, *combinazione* [combination], which is a lot prettier. But there are no 'factions' in my work. There is, I believe, great sincerity. It is a direct enough matter, consequently, which is not at all political. On the contrary, it is humanist…" Masereel was stating that politics is a combination of colliding opinions, whereas art is the mirror of its time. Art is the "habit" within a political climate; not the cultural environment itself, but an expression of a culture's aspirations and its achievements.

Of course, artists cannot deny the influence they have on those around them. Artists may perceive themselves as observers who passively document events around them, but in fact art influences our culture. At its best, political art serves as an early warning system for the health of a culture.

Masereel wrote that "the artist is a witness of his time, but he can also be an accuser, a critic; or he can celebrate in his works the uneasy greatness of his day." As accuser and critic, Masereel excels as the graphic witness of his time.

To understand the context against which each of these wordless books was created, it is useful to consider the literature of its day. A Buddhist philosopher explained that if your topic is so large that it encompasses everything in the world, it is best to start by describing what you are *not* talking about. If you are discussing a room full of furniture and other objects, it would be best to start by saying, *not the chair*. So here is a brief survey of the books that were not allowed. It is what a culture censors that helps describe the moral and political climate of the day.

During the First World War, the U.S. War Department advised the American Library Association to remove any "pacifist" or "disturbing" books from its shelves. *The Espionage Act* of 1917 made it a crime to publish antiwar material. (Charles Schenck was arrested in 1919 for publishing a pamphlet urging men to resist the draft.) In 1929 Jean-Jacques Rousseau's *Confessions* was banned by U.S. customs as "injurious to public morality." In 1930 copies of Voltaire's *Candide* en route to Harvard University were seized by U.S. customs. Nine years later, John Steinbeck's *The Grapes of Wrath* was banned in St. Louis and California for its depiction of the Depression. In Europe, Frans Masereel's books were banned by the Nazis, and many of his contemporaries were arrested or detained for their printmaking activities. James Reid's wordless novel *Life of Christ* was not allowed in the Soviet Union when it was published in 1930 because religious books were tightly controlled. In the 1950s, Lynd Ward was on an FBI list as a "person of interest" because of his socialist views illustrated in such works as *Vertigo* and *Wild Pilgrimage*. Rockwell Kent, who wrote the introduction to Laurence Hyde's wordless novel *Southern Cross*, was subpoenaed by the McCarthy Commission. (Senator McCarthy even had overseas libraries run by the U.S. Information Service pull an anthology of literature from the shelves because it included Henry David Thoreau's *Civil Disobedience*.) Because of U.S. government censorship, you won't find first editions of any of our wordless novels in library rummage sales.

After they were published, wordless books moved quietly through their readers' hands, bearing silent witness to the times in which they were written. Each one of the four wordless novels in this volume looks at the under-

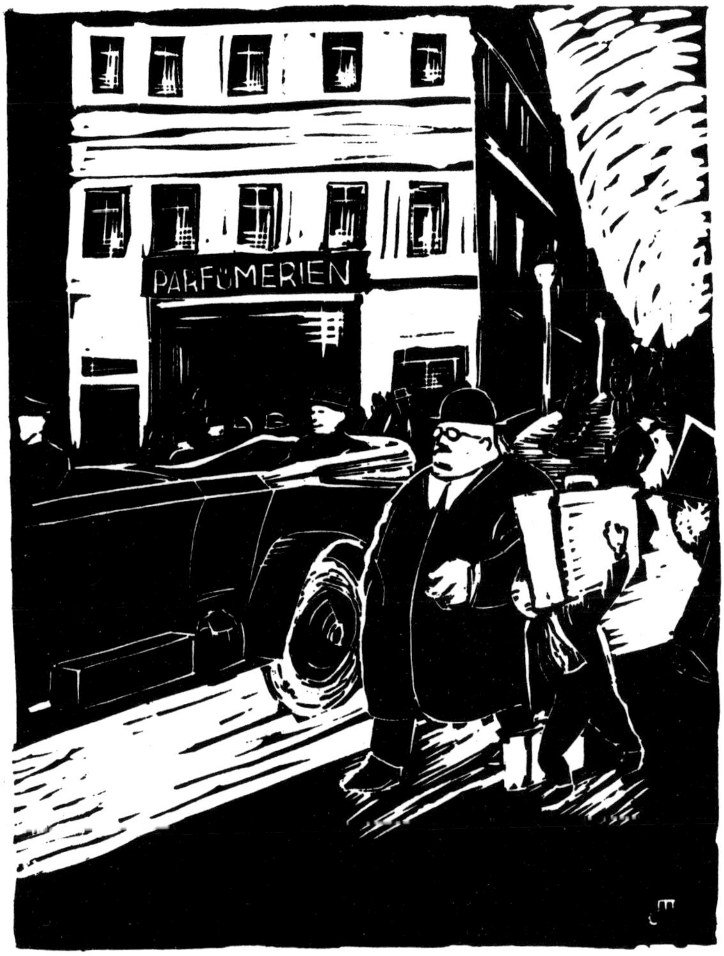
PARFÜMERIEN

This Clément Moreau print, from his book *Erwerbslose Jugend (Youth Without Means),* is a linocut made from battleship linoleum, a burlap-backed flooring material that is often used by artists to make cheap printing blocks. It was popular in the 1930s and 1940s, and many artists including Picasso experimented with it. Parting tools and gouges are the tools of choice for carving linoleum and plank grain woodcuts. Notice the rounded ends of the white lines made by the gouge (illustrated below) in the detail sampled from the sky in the upper right corner of the print.

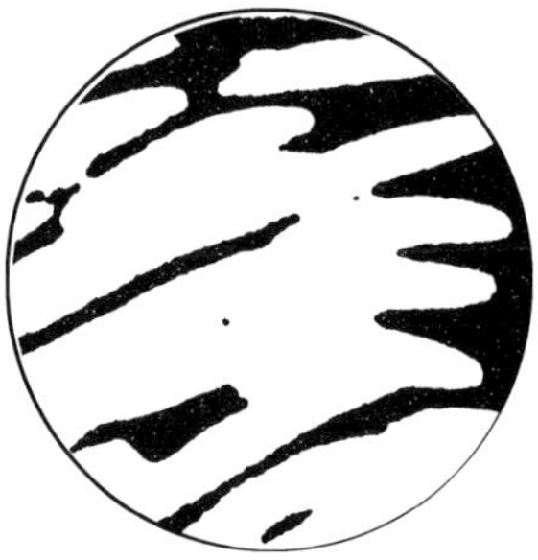

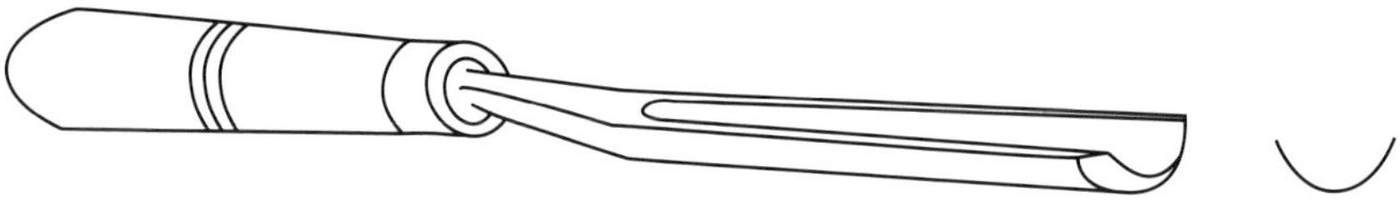

lying and timeless themes of human dignity and social justice. Book arts of this kind share a place in the history of art and are important in showing how social change and political strife challenge the artist.

GRAPHIC WITNESSES IN EUROPE

In 1918 Frans Masereel created his first wordless novel, *25 Images de la Passion d'un Homme* (*The Passion of a Man*), using only 25 wood engravings. It was an immediate success and in the next two years was followed by *Mon Livre d'Heures* (*My Book of Hours*), *Le Soleil* (*The Sun*), *Idée* (*The Idea*) and *Histoire sans Paroles* (*Story Without Words*). These books, and those that followed during his long and productive life, influenced three generations of artists, writers, musicians, animators and filmmakers, yet his work remains largely unknown in North America. Only now is Masereel being rediscovered as one of the most important graphic artists of the 20th century and the father of the modern graphic novel. Masereel's wordless novels have been reprinted in editions published in Japan, China, Eastern Europe, the United States and Canada.

Frans Masereel (1889–1972) was born in Belgium to upper-middle-class parents. He was living in Brittany in August 1914 when the German army marched into Belgium, ushering in the First World War. In 1916 he fled to Paris and later moved to Geneva, where his horror at the slaughter taking place around him led him to join the International Pacifist Movement. Between 1917 and 1918 he created hundreds of individual antiwar drawings and wood engravings.

Masereel moved to Germany in 1923, where he became a close friend of the artist George Grosz, who produced antiwar art similar to Masereel's. Masereel's contact with Romain Rolland, who in 1915 had won the Nobel Prize in literature, introduced him to the ideas of eastern thought and the concepts of a simple lifestyle, similar to what Gandhi embraced. From 1925 to 1927 Masereel created an astonishing collection of more than 800 wood engravings.

During the 1920s Masereel was connected to the Munich-based publisher Kurt Wolff, who released German editions of all Masereel's picture novels. *Die Passion Eines Menschen,* the German edition of *The Passion of*

In this Werner Gothein linoleum print from *The Tightrope Walker and the Clown,* the artist has created tension between his characters with simple white lines and forms. The use of linoleum has its drawbacks — the material can chip and may compress during printing, resulting in the distortion of some lines as shown in the detail. However, this distortion can add character and subtlety to the quality of line that makes a lino print appealing to the eye. The Speedball lino tool pictured below is the most common tool used to create linocuts.

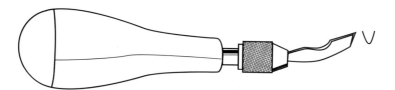

a Man, is the work that is reproduced in this book. It was Wolff's idea to pair up Masereel's wordless novels with introductions by two Nobel Prize winners, Thomas Mann and Hermann Hesse. Thomas Mann wrote the introduction to *Mon Livre d'Heures* and said that Masereel's wood engravings "are a silent film in black and white without titles." Hermann Hesse praised Masereel's *Ideé* and called it a work that captures the essence of the creative process, revealing the struggle that art has to be understood.

When Hitler came to power, Masereel rethought his pacifist position. (All the works published by Kurt Wolff in Munich were banned by the Nazis because they were seen as a degradation of German culture and art.) He tried to join the French army but was turned down because of his age. During the war he spent much of his time avoiding the Nazis and rebelling with the only weapon he had—his art. He fled Paris in 1940 when the Germans invaded and lived in Avignon until 1943, when he again fled because his life was in danger. After the war ended he was able to resume his creative life and accepted a teaching position at the Arts Center in Saarbrücken, Belgium. He began having international exhibitions of his work in Paris, New York and Mexico. Throughout the 1950s and 60s Masereel's work took on more optimistic themes, and his reputation grew internationally. He expanded his creative horizons, designing costumes for numerous theater productions, and continued his creative work well into his 80s. Frans Masereel died in Ghent in 1972 and is immortalized through the graphics art center that bears his name in Kasterlee, Belgium.

The 1930s and 40s saw a burst of other wordless novels, inspired by Masereel, in Germany and elsewhere in Europe. Helena Bocharakova (1894–1980) was a Czechoslovakian artist known for her wordless book *Childhood: A Cycle of Woodcuts,* published in 1931. Bocharakova studied art in Prague, graduating in 1922 with a scholarship to study art in Paris, where she may have been exposed to Masereel's wordless novels. Her books are extremely rare. She always included the word "cycle" in her series of prints, to indicate that they were a series reflecting a theme and not meant to be read as individual visual narratives.

The German Expressionist Werner Gothein (1890–1968) produced a wordless novel in 1949, *The Tightrope Walker and the Clown* (*Die Seiltänzerin und ihr Clown*), with 102 woodcuts in a limited edition of 500 copies. Gothein was part of the Expressionist group of artists known as The Bridge ("Die Brücke"), which believed in greater artistic freedom from the establish-

This lead engraving by Otto Nückel is taken from his wordless novel *Destiny*. The detail shows Nückel's extensive use of the lining tool (shown below), which creates multiple white lines with a single stroke. This effect creates the illusion of grays in the image, resulting in a greater depth of shading and subtle contrasts.

ment and was influenced by African art. He studied under Ernst Ludwig Kirchner, the best known member of the group, whose works were defamed by the Nazis as degenerate. Kirchner committed suicide in 1938. Gothein continued to work throughout the war and was inspired by Expressionist printmaking.

Carl Meffert (1903–1988) changed his name to Clément Moreau when he lost his papers while fleeing Germany and the Nazis in 1933. A student of the Expressionist artist Käthe Kollwitz, his *Youth Without Means* (*Erwerbslose Jugend,* 1928, with a foreword by Kollwitz) was made up of six autobiographical linocuts depicting his poverty and incarceration for theft. These were a prelude to his later works about the injustice he suffered at the hands of the authorities. Meffert's short picture narratives provide us with a glimpse into the social upheaval in Germany during the 1930s.

Otto Nückel (1888–1956) first studied medicine before deciding on a career in the visual arts. He moved to Munich, where he joined the artist group known as the Secession. His wordless novel *Destiny* examined the social issues surrounding poverty, alcoholism, women's rights and child poverty. *Destiny* was published in 1930. One can't help but wonder if Nückel was influenced by Fritz Lang's film of the same name—both with victimized women as protagonists—that was screened in Germany in 1921. Because of the expense of wood, Nückel used lead for engraving. Lead is easily recycled, so if the engraver makes a mistake the material can be melted down and used again. A slip of the graver on a piece of wood means the work is ruined and the block must be resurfaced or discarded. Whether an engraver chooses lead or wood, the two surfaces print identically.

Lynd Ward mentions in his book, *Storyteller Without Words,* that he believes Nückel surpasses Masereel with his plot development and subtle psychological interplay between characters. But although Nückel shows greater technical depth in his engravings, Masereel shows more originality in his plot.

GRAPHIC WITNESSES IN NORTH AMERICA

In North America, the wordless novel developed as a popular medium of expression, thanks to the influence largely of Masereel and Nückel. James Reid (1907–1989) created his only wordless novel, *The Life of Christ,* in 1930.

Part of what unifies any sequential narrative is the style of the art carried through the story. Much of the style in an artist's wood engraving is dictated by the choice of tools used. In this engraving from *The Life of Christ*, James Reid has chosen the engraver's chisel (illustrated below) to create the rectangular spikes that protrude from the cacti. The enlarged detail is sampled from the cacti just below the devil's ear. Although Reid has used other tools to create this engraving, it is his use of the chisel here that makes this image remarkable.

Inspired by the many early block book picture narratives of the life of Christ, Reid attempted to portray this epic story with only 71 images. A review of the work in *Time* magazine commented that "he labors under the difficulty that faces all modern portraitists of Christ: either to be original at the risk of irreverence or heresy, or traditional without originality." Reid's work, with its art deco style, is original. Reid has not given us a simple interpretation of the life of Christ, but a retelling of the mood and atmosphere written in wood. His engravings, with their elongated figures and their dramatic postures, seem to be influenced by Rockwell Kent. Reid was born in Philadelphia, where he lived his entire life. Most of his illustrations are for children's books. *The Life of Christ* is a spiritually motivated book and not a religious one.

Giacomo Patri (1898–1978) was an Italian-born American who lived in San Francisco, where he worked as an illustrator and a teacher. After the Second World War, Patri began teaching at the California Labor School. Of that school, with its pro-labor agenda, Patri commented, "It was there that my contact with the working man developed my philosophy that the human organism is essentially a creative unit." The school was closed in the 1950s, when pressure from the McCarthy hearings made it impossible for it to function. Patri created his masterpiece, *White Collar* (1938), as a statement on the divide between white-collar and blue-collar workers. This work is an autobiographical account of Patri's early struggles as a commercial artist. Although he did not lose his home to a mortgage company (as happens to his protagonist), he had friends who did.

During the 1930s, many white-collar workers in the United States refused to join labor unions. Patri describes how this book came about:

> One day a friend handed me a paper proclaiming a solution to the all-pervasive social and economic problems. Naturally I became very excited. I wanted to be part of a movement that promised to solve our desperate situation ... *White Collar* was to be my contribution to, what I believed then, an indispensable understanding of the necessity of unity among all American workers and voters. I was not a writer, so illustrations in sequence were, I thought, the answer.

White Collar is one of the gems of wordless novels. Through 120 linoleum cuts it documents the 1929 stock market crash and the crisis that followed. The first copies were hand done (1939–39) and bound by Giacomo and

The parting tool (shown below) is a favorite among linocut artists, because it offers them a variety of line widths in a single tool. When the parting tool cuts into the lino, it can create a tapered white line or a white line of equal width (as shown in the detail). This Giacomo Patri linocut taken from *White Collar* is an excellent example of the parting tool's range and flexibility. The white dots in the background were probably created with a sharp, pointed tool similar to an awl.

his wife Stella (1896-2001) with help from their young sons. Stella Nicole Patri later became an internationally recognized master bookbinder, making the first copies of *White Collar* an important record of her developing bookbinding skills. A larger edition was published by the Pisani Printing Company in 1940. The book was first used as a promotional piece by the labor movement to show how white-collar workers were as much in danger of unfair labor practices as the so-called blue collar workers. It had an epilogue by John L. Lewis of the United Mine Workers of America and an introduction by Rockwell Kent, who commented, "Into the darkness of depression it throws light; the tragic dissonances it resolves; and to the dead hope it brings resurrection."

White Collar was reviewed by wood engraver and wordless novelist Lynd Ward in the February 1941 issue of the *Office and Professional Workers News*. All the images were cut into linoleum, a cheap flooring material, and printed by hand on Patri's letterpress. The only wordless book made by Patri, it took him almost three years to complete. Patri later established his own art school in San Francisco, which offered courses from 1948 to 1966. Besides being an accomplished printmaker and illustrator, he was also a champion fencer. Perhaps that expertise explains his fine cutting technique in linoleum.

Because of his influence on later American artists and the power and breadth of his work, Lynd Kendall Ward (1905–85) is among the best known of the wordless novelists. His first, highly successful book, *God's Man,* was followed by *Madman's Drum,* published in 1930 to great acclaim. Four other wordless novels followed, including *Wild Pilgrimage.* The Great Depression was the most prolific period for American artists working in the medium of print, which addressed the social and labor issues of the times. Lynd Ward was one of the founders of the Equinox Cooperative Press, which was dedicated to noncommercial artwork, and the American Artists Union.

Ward was born in Chicago, where his father was a Methodist minister and political activist. He went to college at Columbia Teachers' College in New York. He married May McNeer shortly after graduating, and the couple set off for Germany so Lynd could study at the National Academy of Graphic Art in Leipzig. There his interest in wood engraving was honed under the tutelage of the master wood engraver Hans Mueller. It was in a Leipzig bookshop that Ward discovered Frans Masereel and became immediately inspired by the format of the wordless novel format. In Ward's

Lynd Ward's use of the spitsticker (or elliptic tint tool as it is more commonly known in North America) can be seen in this print from *Wild Pilgrimage.* The detail, taken from just above the ear to the right, shows Ward's use of crosshatching and the fine white lines that curve gracefully to express the old man's thin hair. Ward has also used a stipple technique with the spitsticker that adds variety and atmosphere to this dramatic wood engraving.

autobiographical book, *Storyteller Without Words,* he reflects on how Frans Masereel and Otto Nückel influenced his work.

When the Wards returned from Germany in 1927, Lynd immediately began working on his first wordless novel, *God's Man.* He created 139 engravings that told the story of a struggling artist who sells his soul without reading the fine print. *God's Man* was released in October 1929—the week the New York Stock Market crashed, marking the beginning of the Great Depression. Although not the best time for launching a book, *God's Man* was in its third printing by January 1930. The book sold over 20,000 copies in four years and introduced America to the wordless novel.

Wild Pilgrimage (1932), Ward's third book, is one of his most challenging and creative pieces. He touches on the issues of racism, love and rejection, and power and class structure in the labor movement. Through 98 wood engravings it tells the story of the crushing city, and of how one man's wandering takes him into the darkness of the inner consciousness as he tries to make sense of an unfair world. Ward describes the book:

> In the American experience there is probably no more basic or recurrent impulse than to leave society. It is a madness—or a sanity—that can take hold of any citizen when the daily grind becomes suddenly more abrasive than anyone should be asked to endure; when the crush of too many people in too small a space is finally more than one can take; when the noise and smells of the city are at last too stifling to be borne. Then the urge to pick up and leave, to get away somehow, is irresistible. Surely, the impulse whispers in your ear, it is not inevitable that I should live and die in this hellhole; surely, there is more to the world and to life than this.

Lynd Ward's wordless novels made between 1929 and 1937 are important for anyone interested in the art and artists of the Great Depression. These books not only defined the concerns of the time, but also considered the circumstances that created them. From the Hoovervilles to Roosevelt's New Deal, Ward takes us through those years. Today we have the luxury to reflect on the impact those times have had on politics and art. Lynd Ward is truly one of the most important artists of his time. Allen Ginsberg credits Ward's wordless novels as the inspiration for his epic poem "Howl." The contemporary American wood engraver Michael McCurdy brought

In this engraving from his novel *Southern Cross*, Laurence Hyde has used a menagerie of pattern and line to give us his impression of an atom bomb explosion. From the quality of his white lines, we can determine what engraving tool he used for certain effects. The graver (or burin) pictured below can engrave white lines that move from thin to thick. The detail, taken from the sky in the top left of the image, shows how the white lines taper, adding an upwards movement to the sky.

Ginsberg and Ward together in 1978 to produce a limited edition broadside, which featured a Lynd Ward engraving of Ginsberg's "Moloch." Michael McCurdy inherited Lynd Ward's engraving tools after Ward's death in 1985 — the sword handed to the next generation.

Laurence Hyde (1914–87) was born in England at the beginning of the First World War. His family moved to Canada in 1926, settling in Toronto in 1928. Hyde studied art and later joined the National Film Board of Canada. Legend has it that he landed his job at the National Film Board by showing the managing director proofs from his wordless novel *Southern Cross* (1951). Hyde's work was indication enough that he understood sequential art and its relationship to motion pictures and the storyboard. The transition to filmmaking would be easy, and he was hired on the spot.

Laurence Hyde is the only post–World War II artist featured in this book. His work is a definitive marker of the Cold War years. Rockwell Kent's introduction to *Southern Cross* provides a nice link between Patri's Depression era visual narrative and Hyde's contemporary fear of global destruction. Through 120 wood engravings, *Southern Cross* criticizes the U.S government for testing hydrogen bombs at the Bikini Atoll in 1946. As Rockwell Kent wrote in his introduction, "The bomb, that steel-clad dove of peace, is lowered to the ocean floor. The zero hour nears. A finger presses on the key. And to the island that was Eden, to every living creature but one child of man, to the birds of the air, to the fish of the sea, comes on blinding flash the everlasting peace of death."

THERE ARE VERY FEW ARTISTS today using wood engraving, linocut or woodcut to illustrate their narratives, since photocopiers and the computer are more accessible forms of publishing than blocks of wood and iron presses. Still, artists are rediscovering the art of storytelling through the work of Frans Masereel, Giacomo Patri, Lynd Ward, Laurence Hyde and other wordless novelists. Hopefully the works reproduced in this volume will inspire present and future artists, and will provide an awareness and appreciation of the cultural impact that these wordless novels had and continue to have.

Enough said. These are works to be appreciated without any more words, but with reflection and silent delight.

FRANS MASEREEL

DIE PASSION EINES MENSCHEN

(THE PASSION OF A MAN)

DIE PASSION EINES MENSCHEN

25 HOLZSCHNITTE V. FRANS MASEREEL

BEI KURT WOLFF MUENCHEN

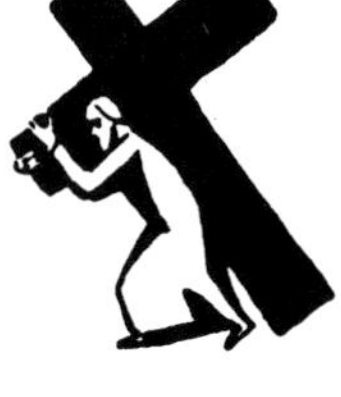

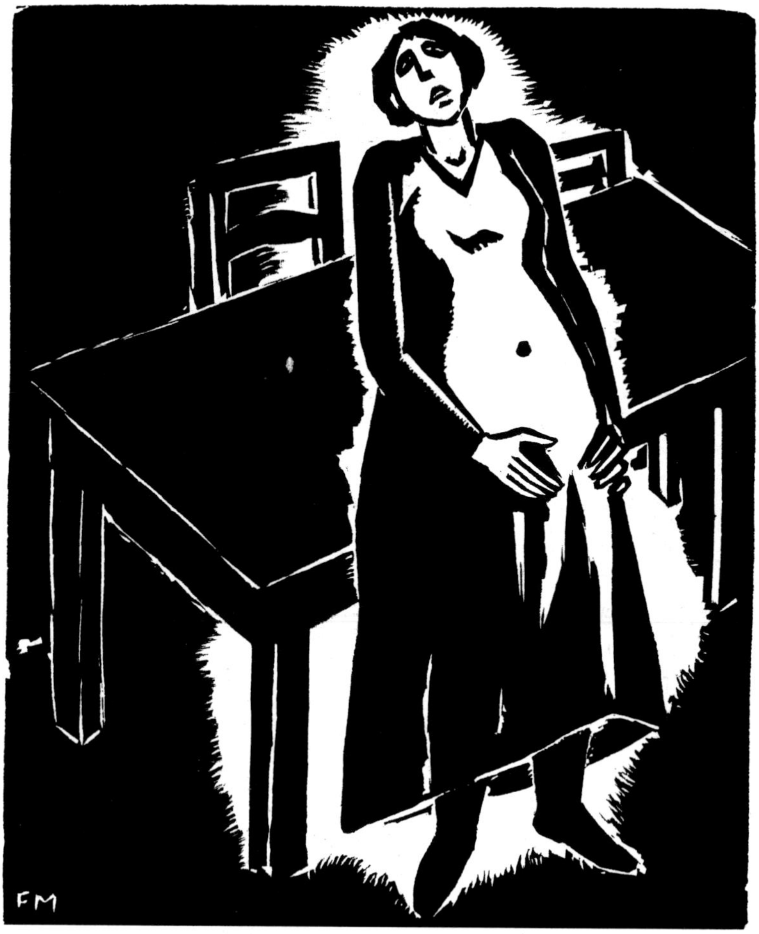
FM

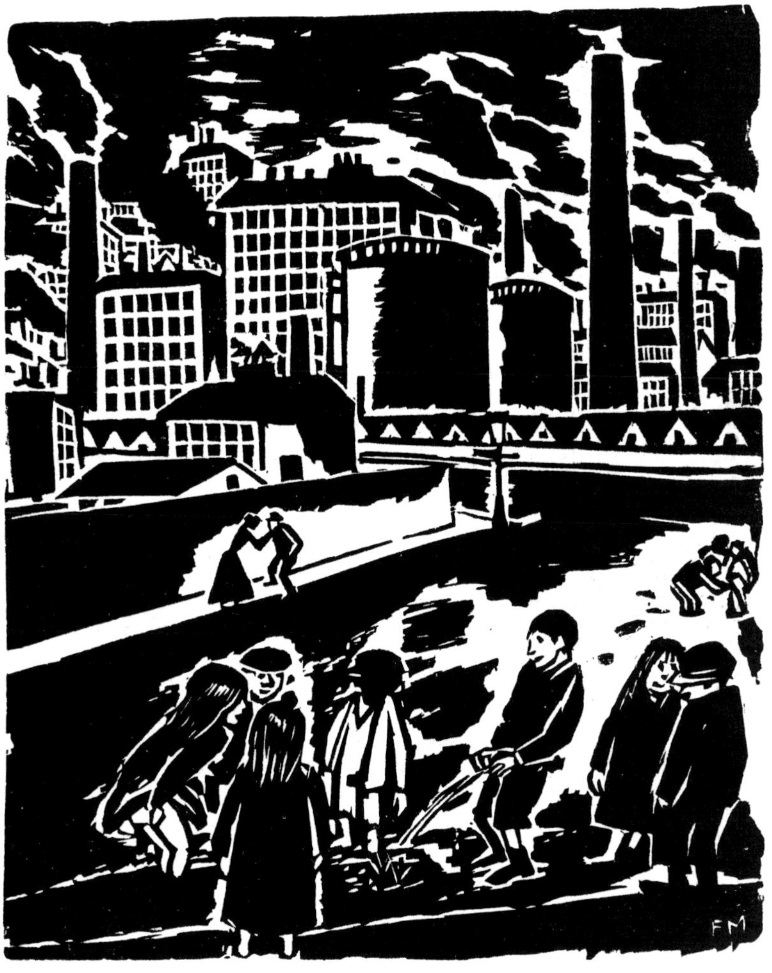
FM

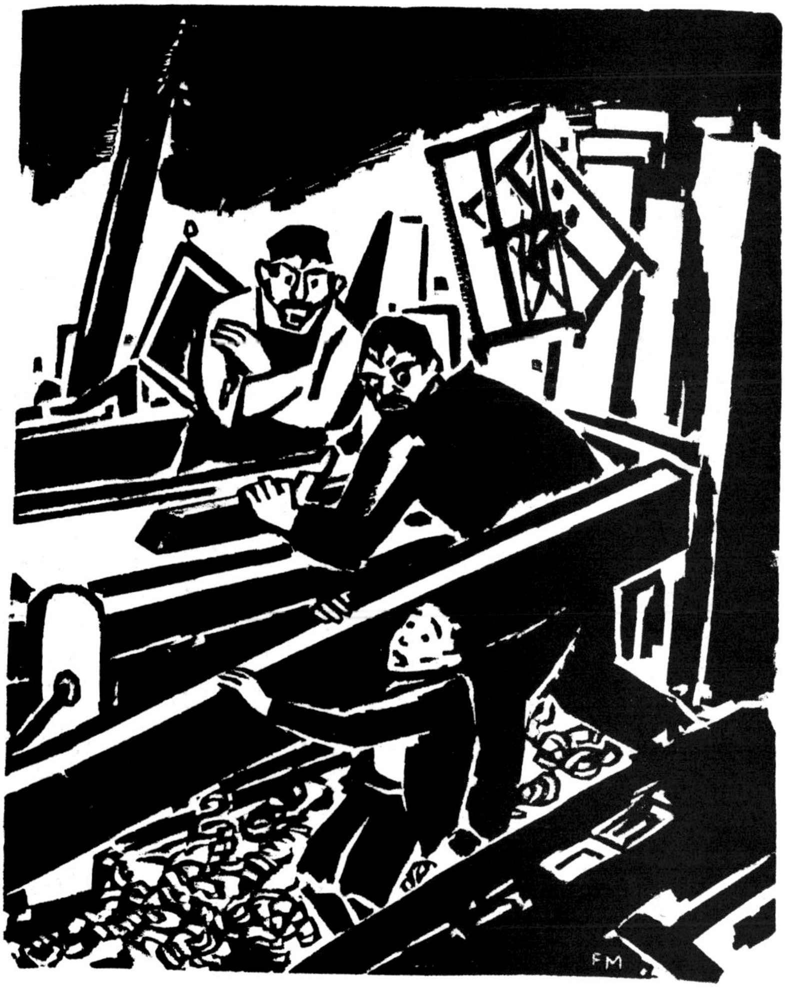
FM

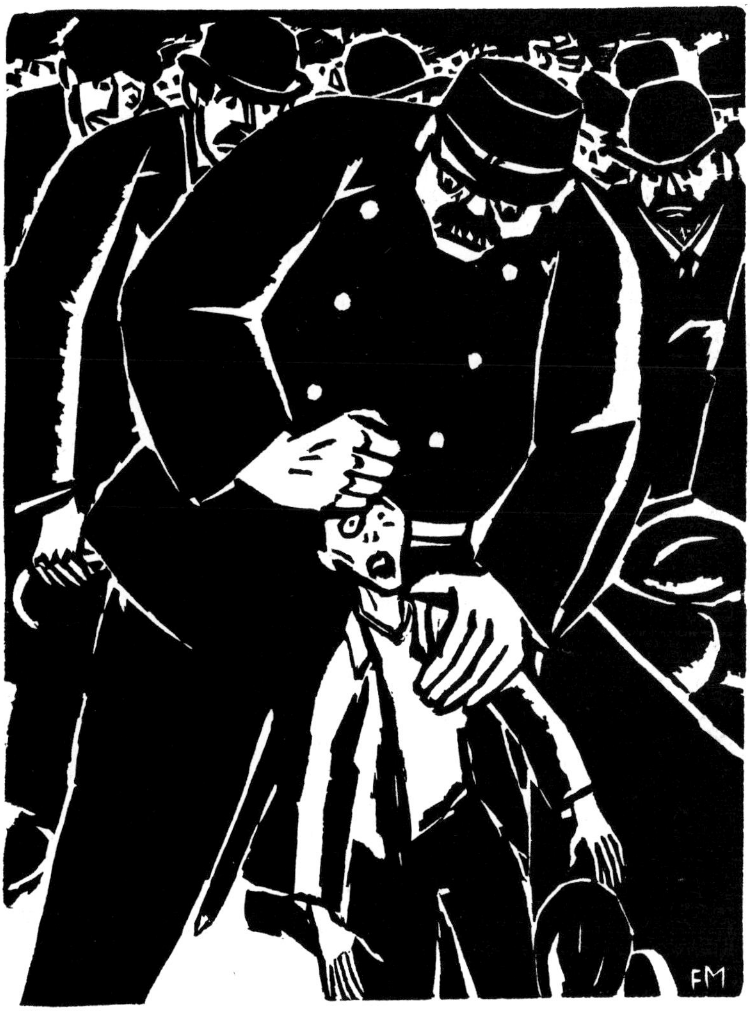
FM

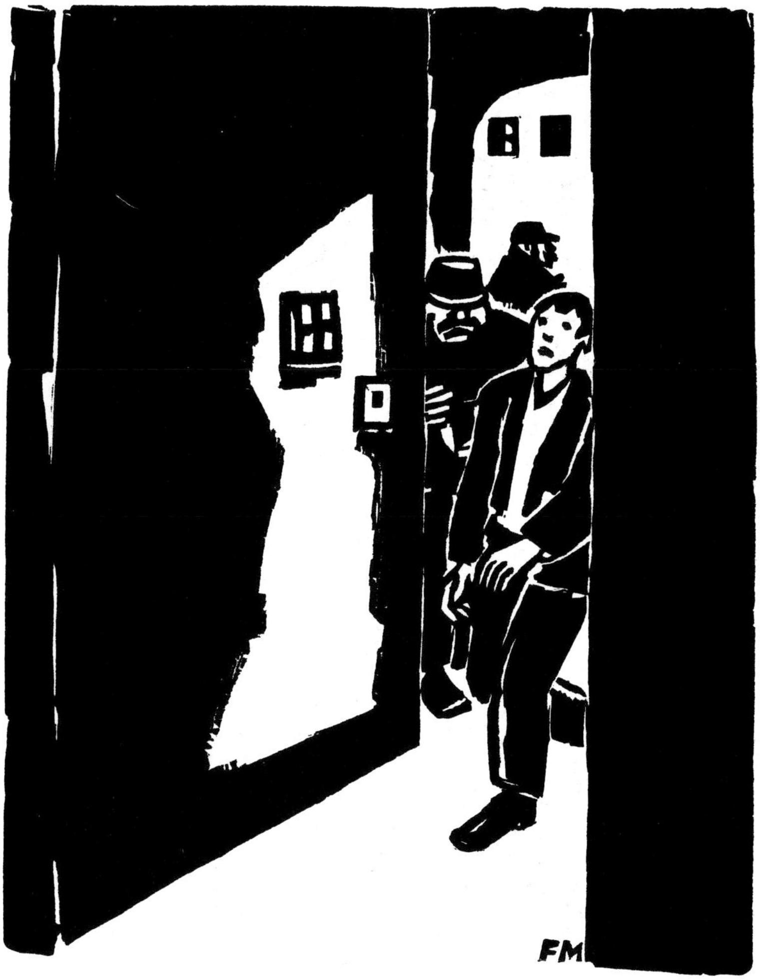
FM

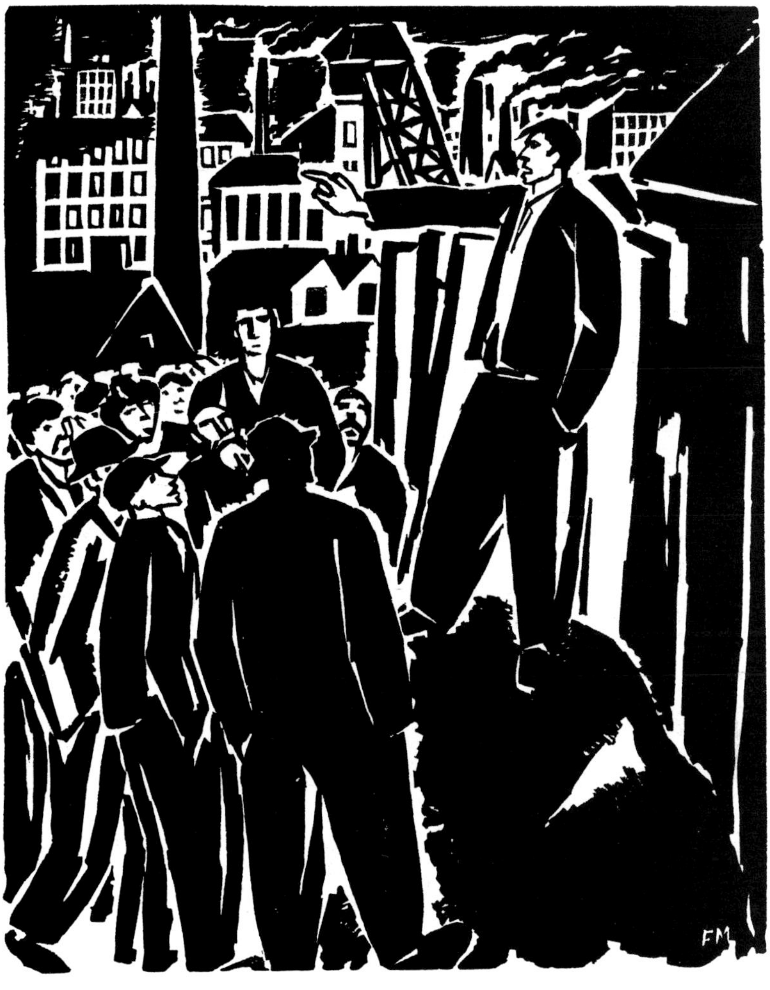
FM

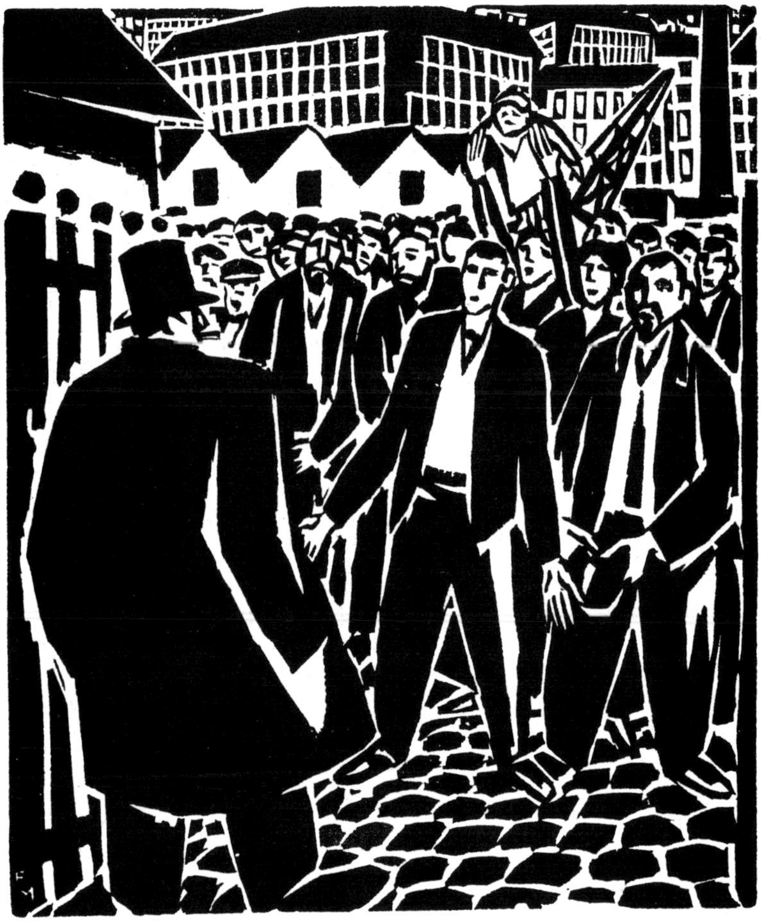
F M

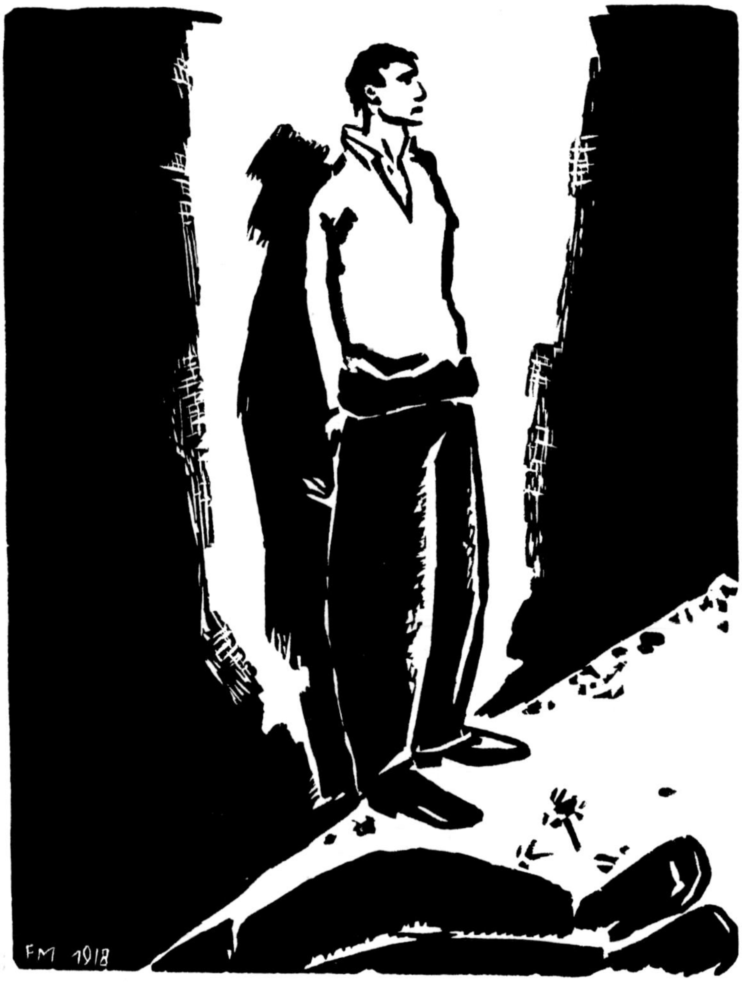
FM 1918

LYND WARD

WILD PILGRIMAGE

NOVELS IN WOOD CUTS BY LYND WARD

GODS' MAN, MADMAN'S DRUM, WILD PILGRIMAGE

HARRISON SMITH & ROBERT HAAS

WILD PILGRIMAGE

NEW YORK
1 9 3 2

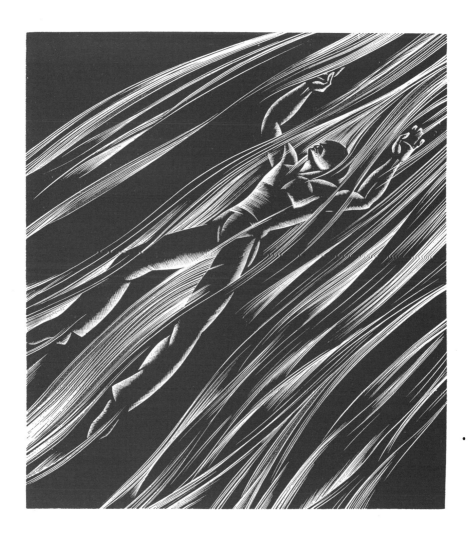

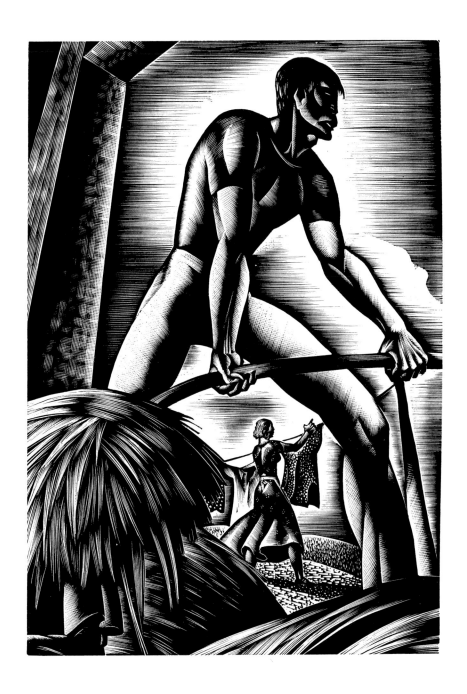

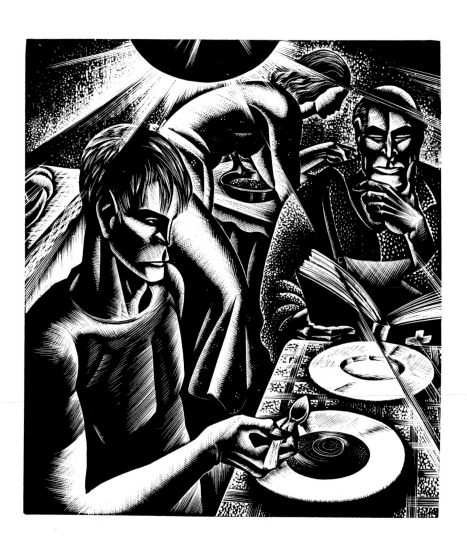

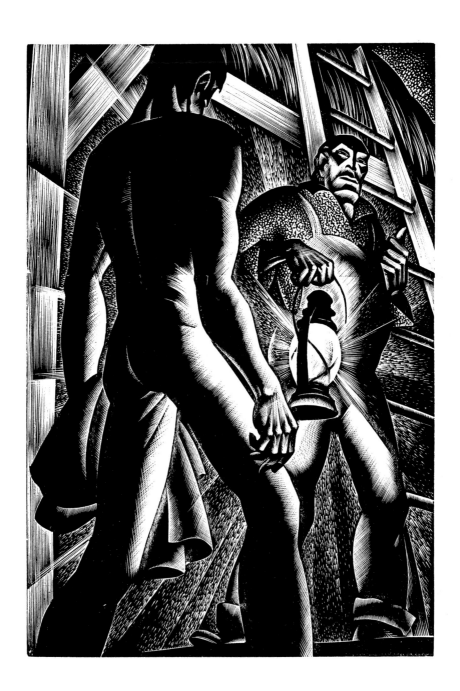

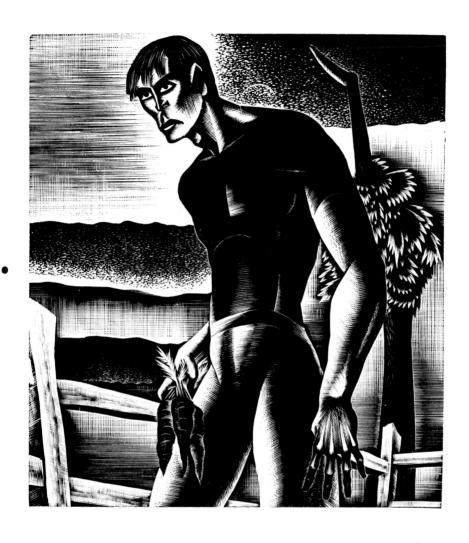

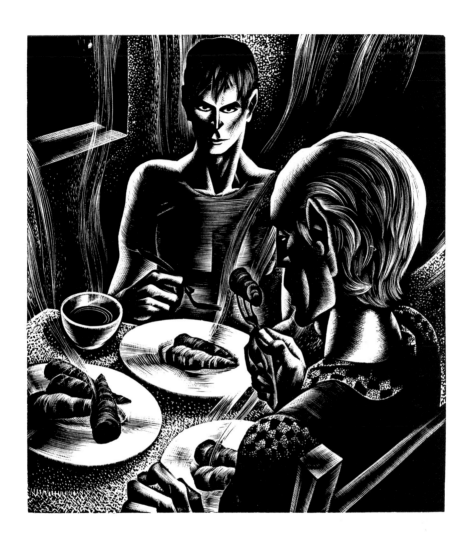

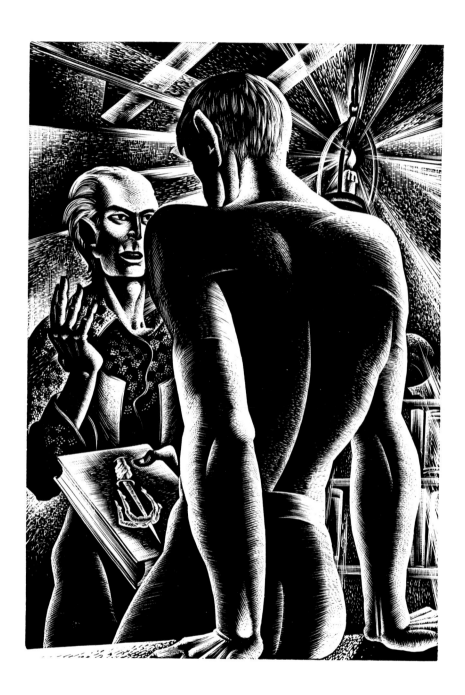

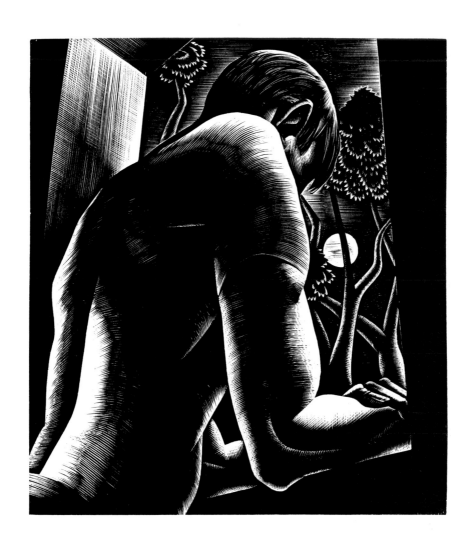

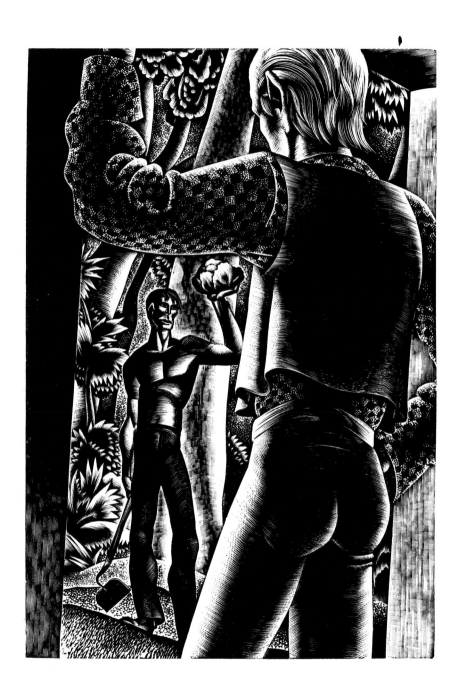

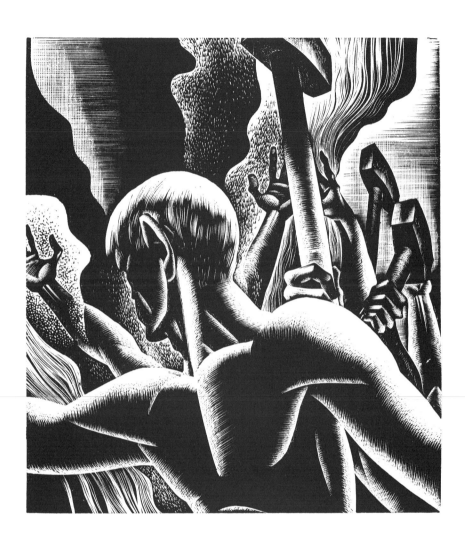

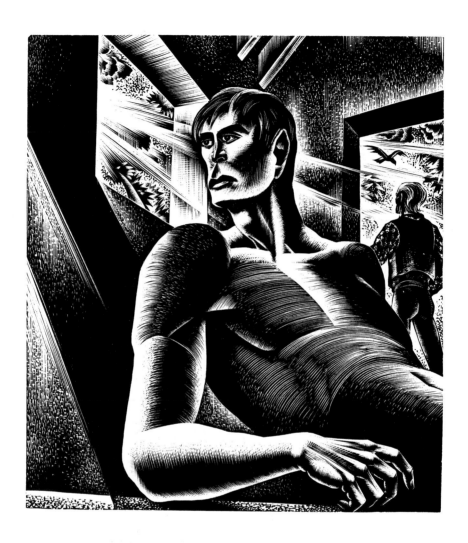

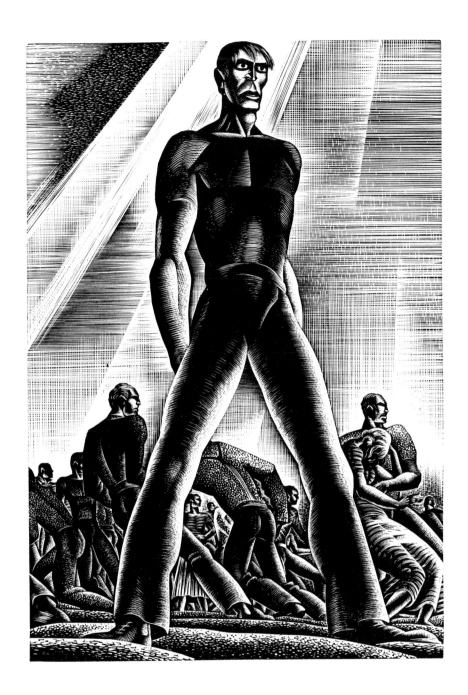

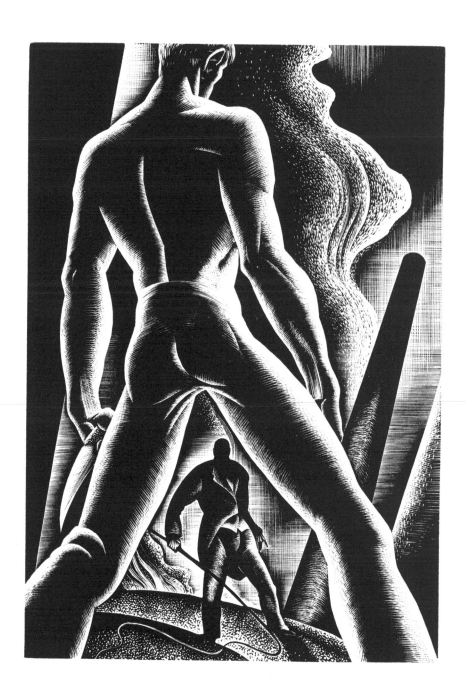

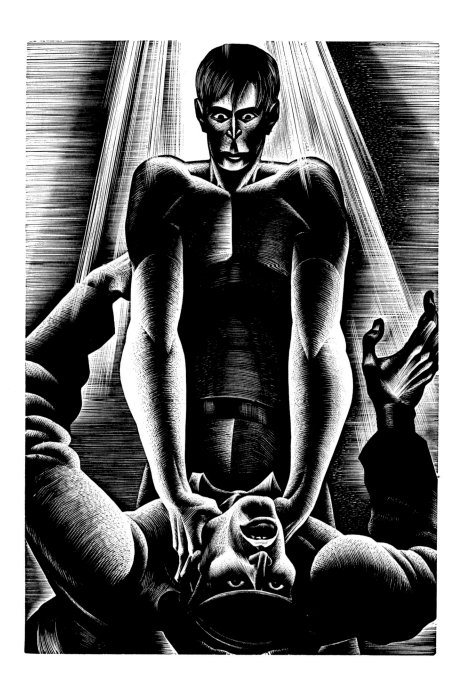

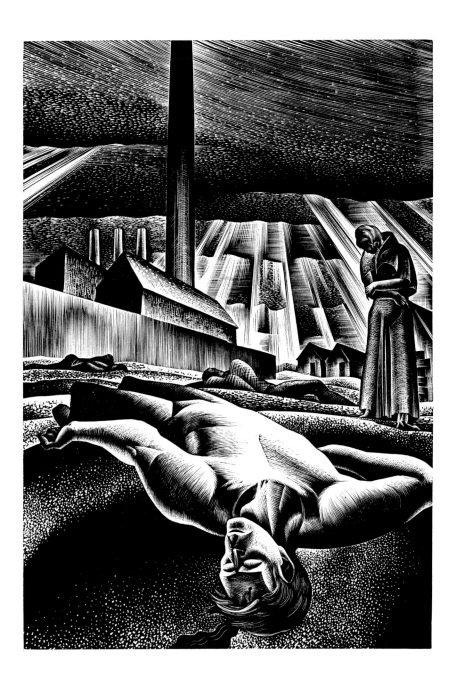

GIACOMO PATRI

WHITE COLLAR

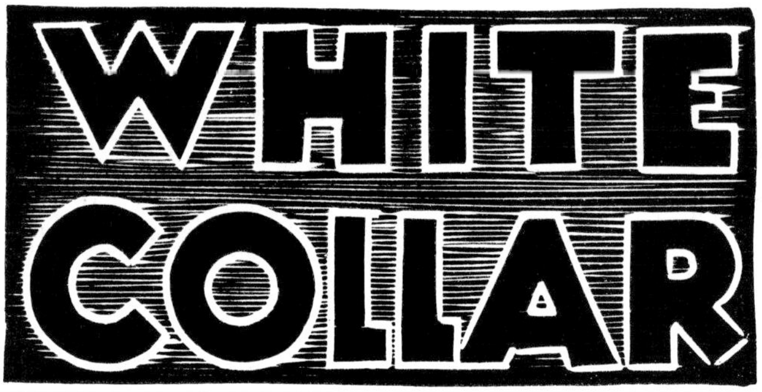
WHITE
COLLAR

NOVEL IN LINOCUTS
BY GIACOMO PATRI

GIACOMO PATRI

THE CLIMB
TO SUCCESS

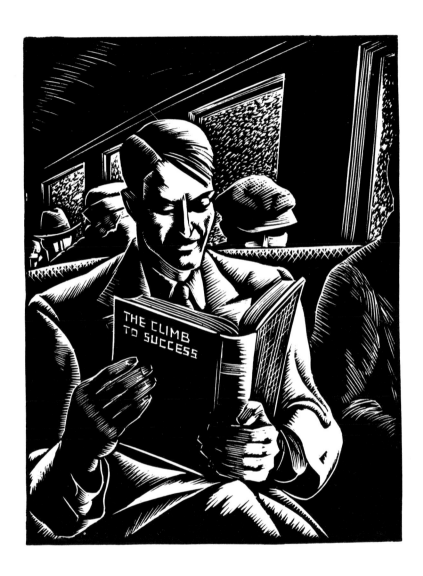

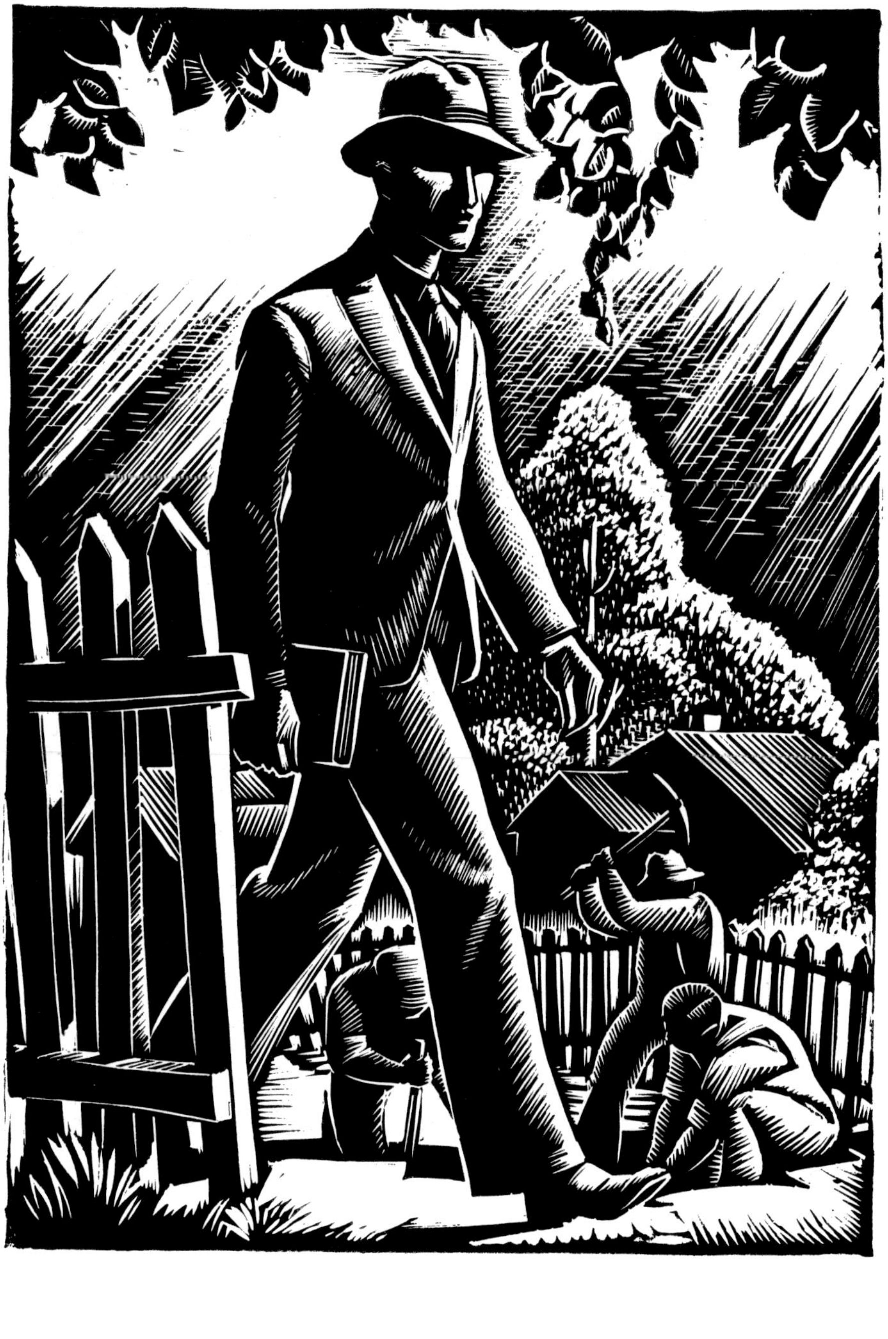

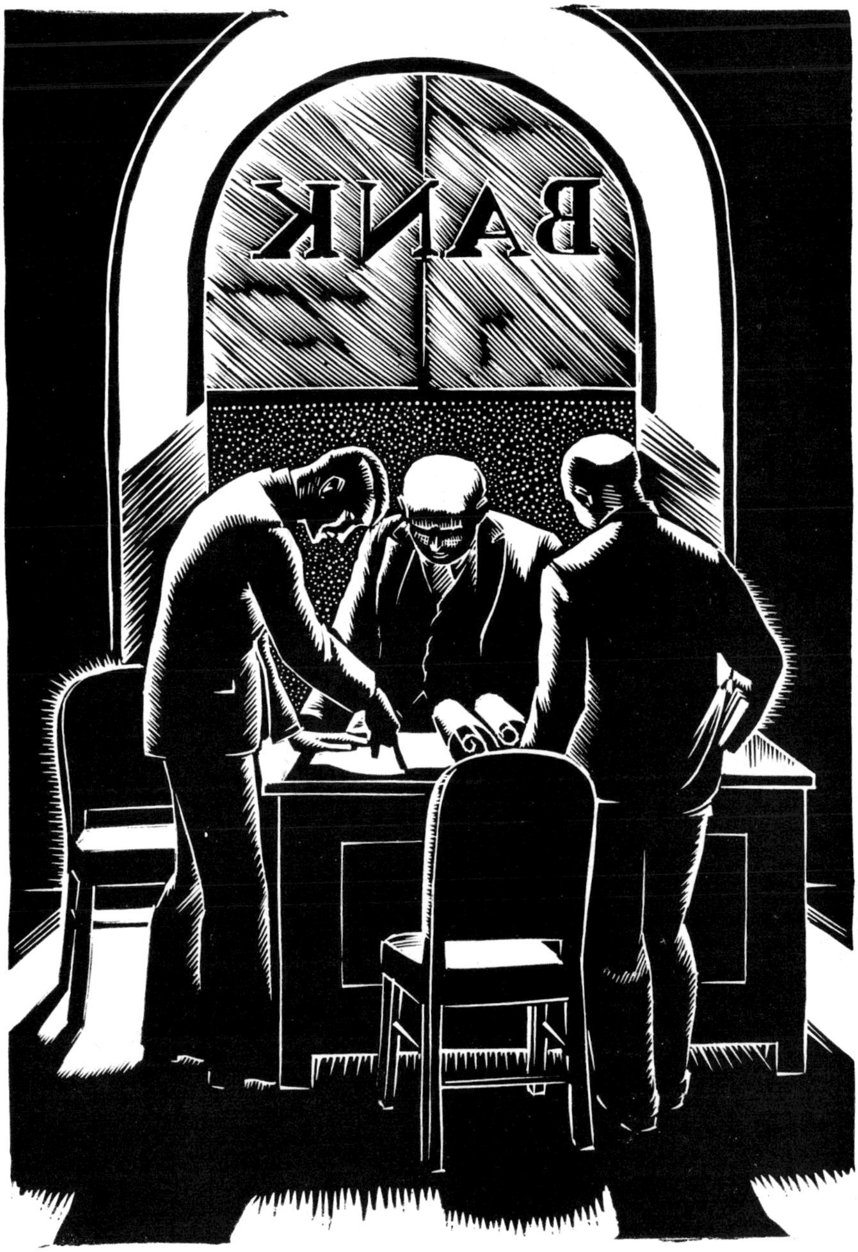
BANK

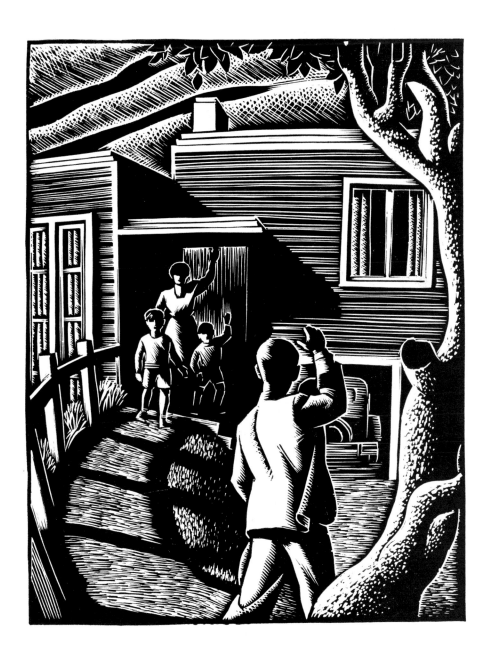

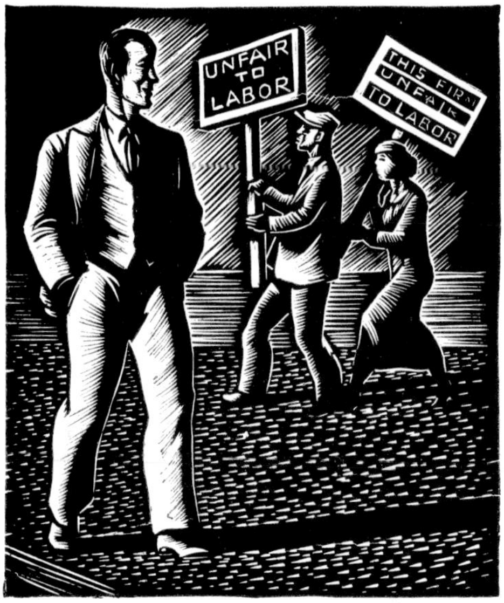
UNFAIR TO LABOR
THIS FIRM UNFAIR TO LABOR

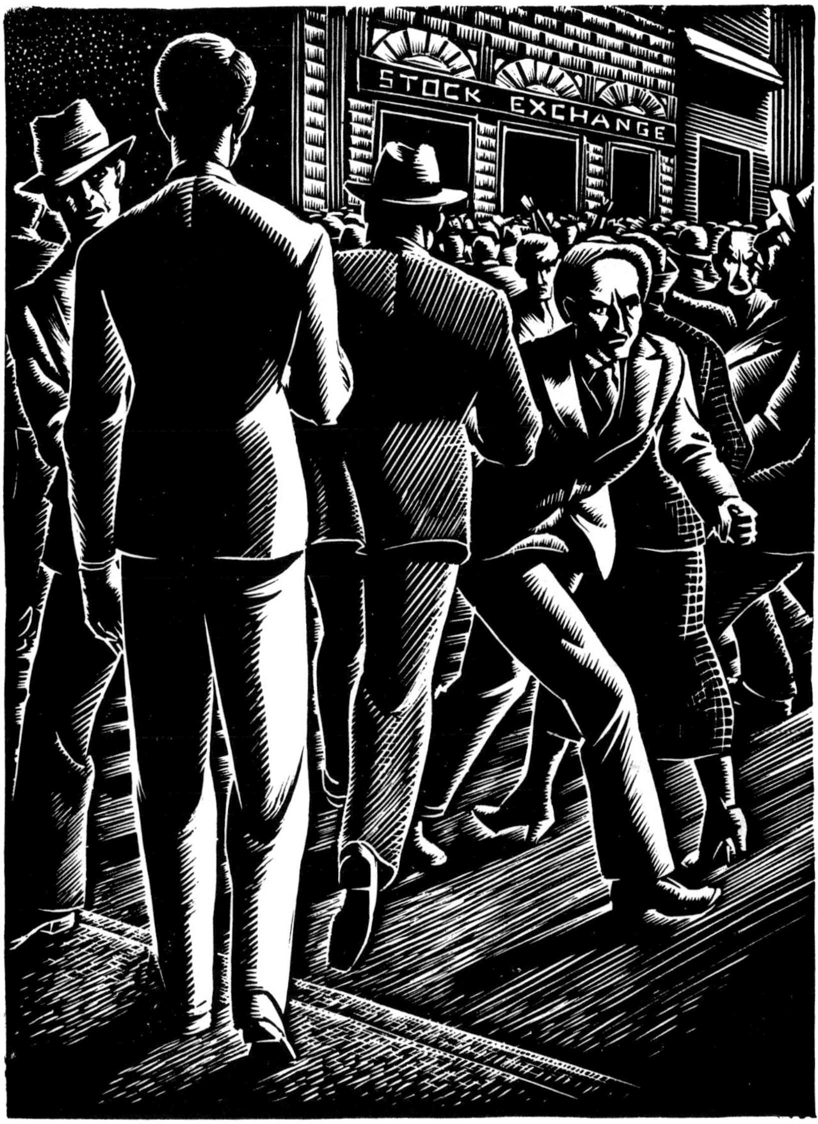
STOCK EXCHANGE

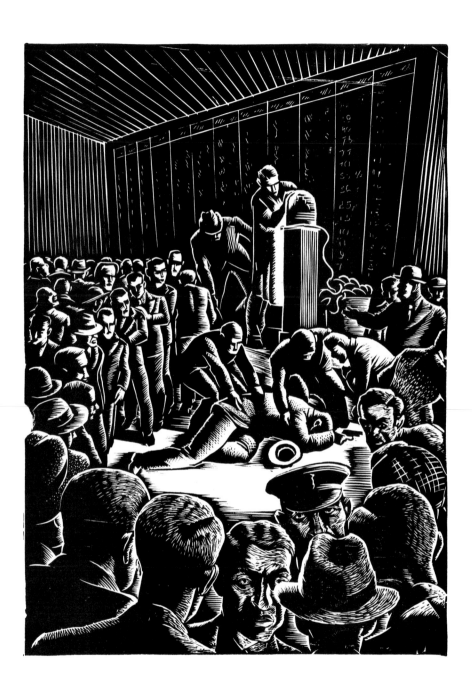

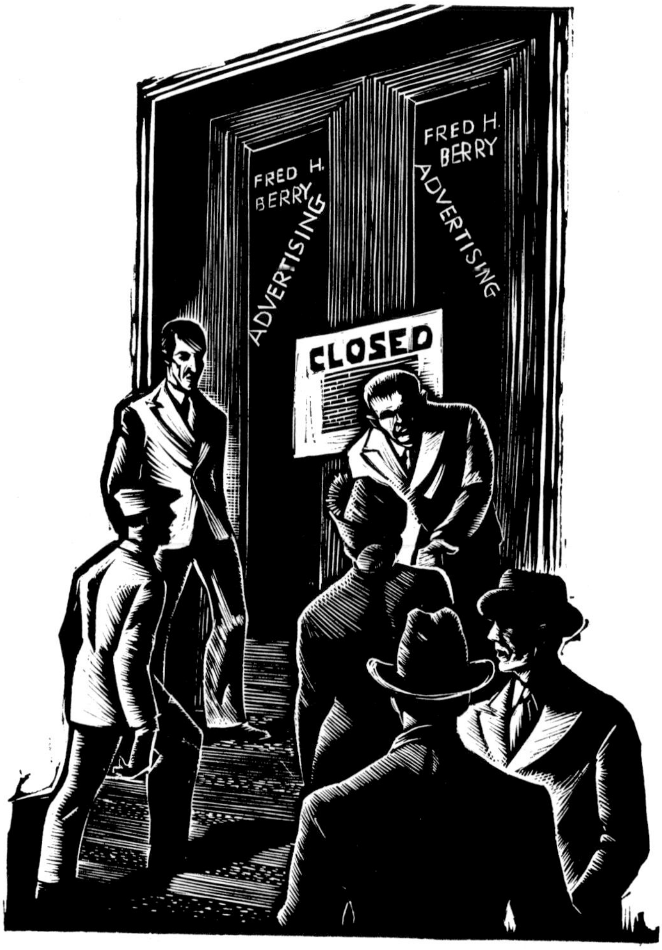
FRED H. BERRY
ADVERTISING
FRED H. BERRY
ADVERTISING
CLOSED

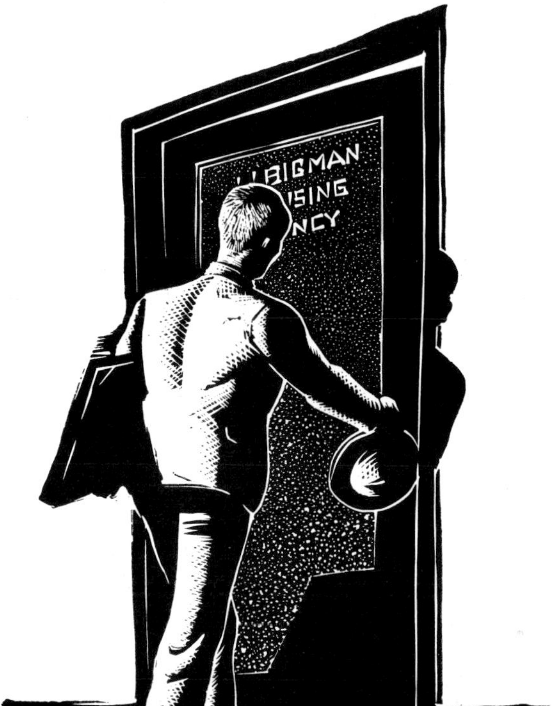
BIGMAN
ISING
NCY

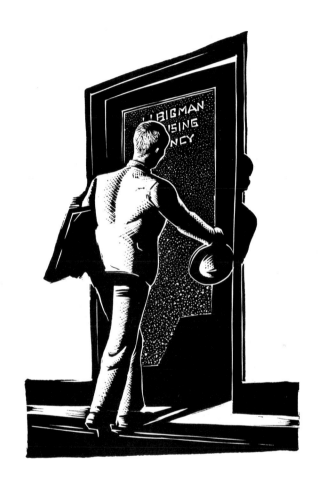

GIACOMO PATRI

GIACOMO PATRI

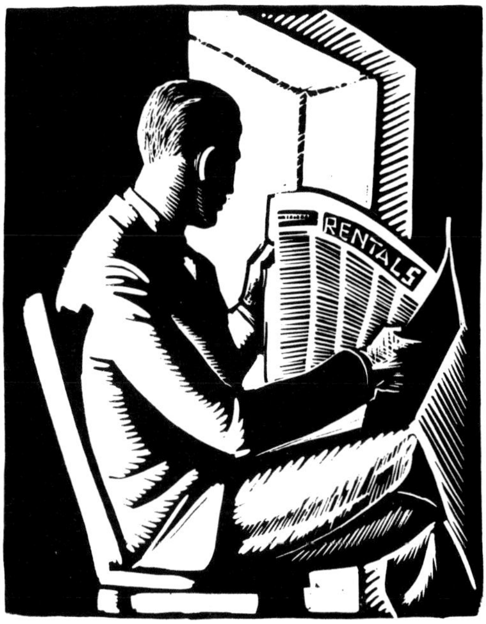
RENTALS

GIACOMO PATRI

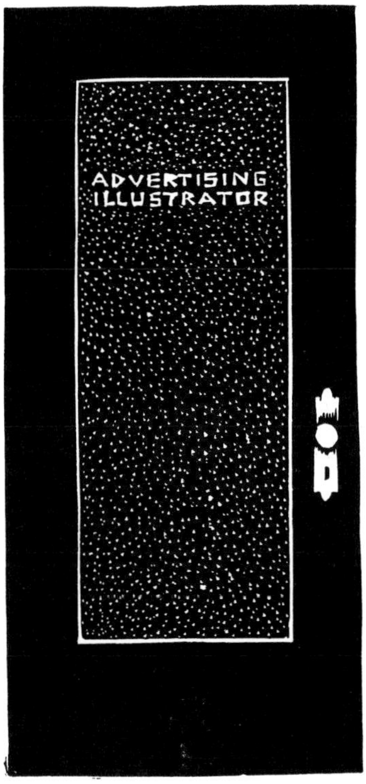
ADVERTISING
ILLUSTRATOR

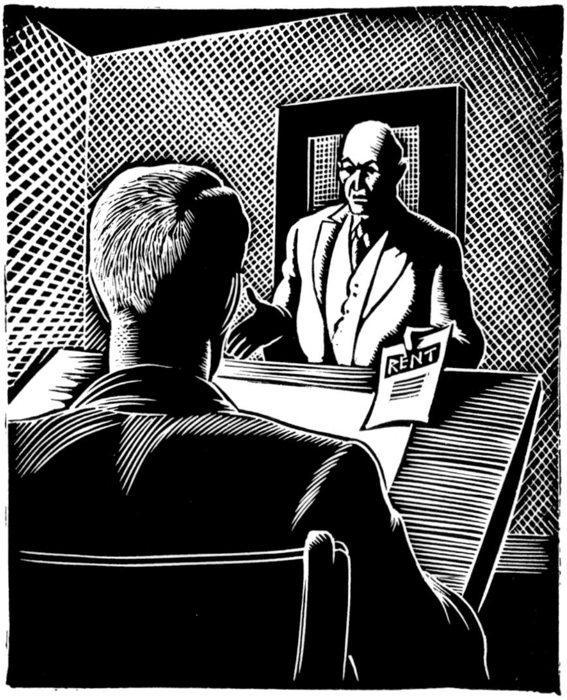
RENT

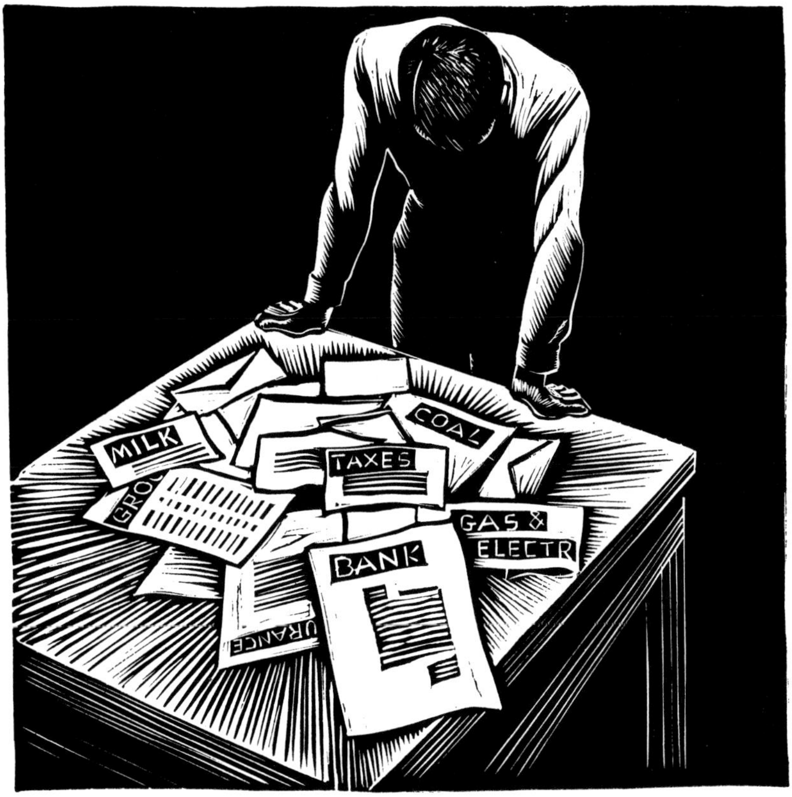
MILK
COAL
TAXES
GRO
GAS &
ELECTR
BANK
URANCE

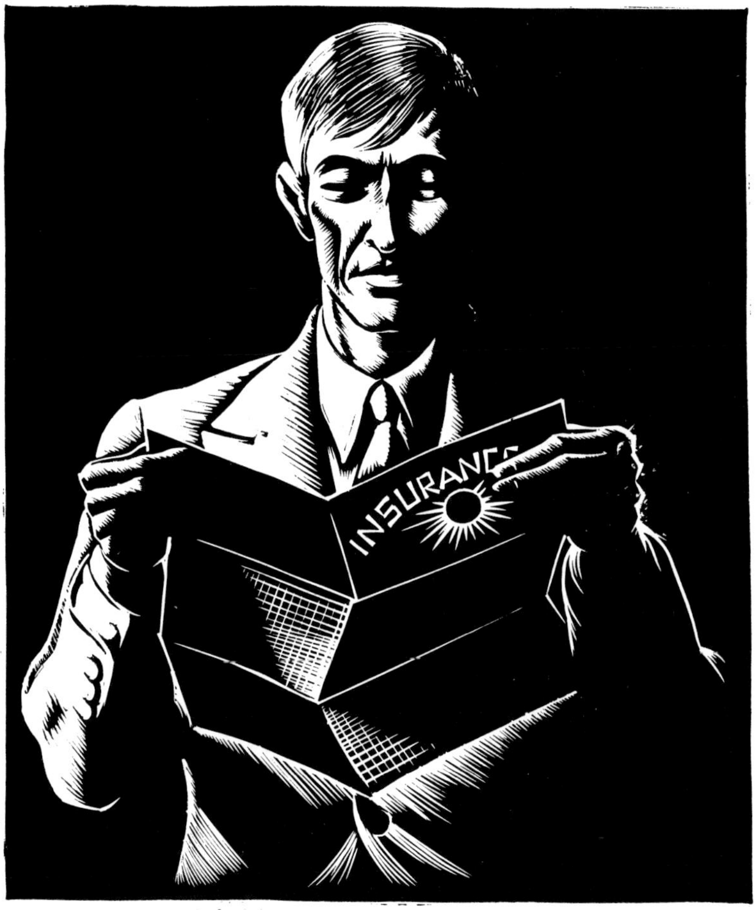
INSURANCE

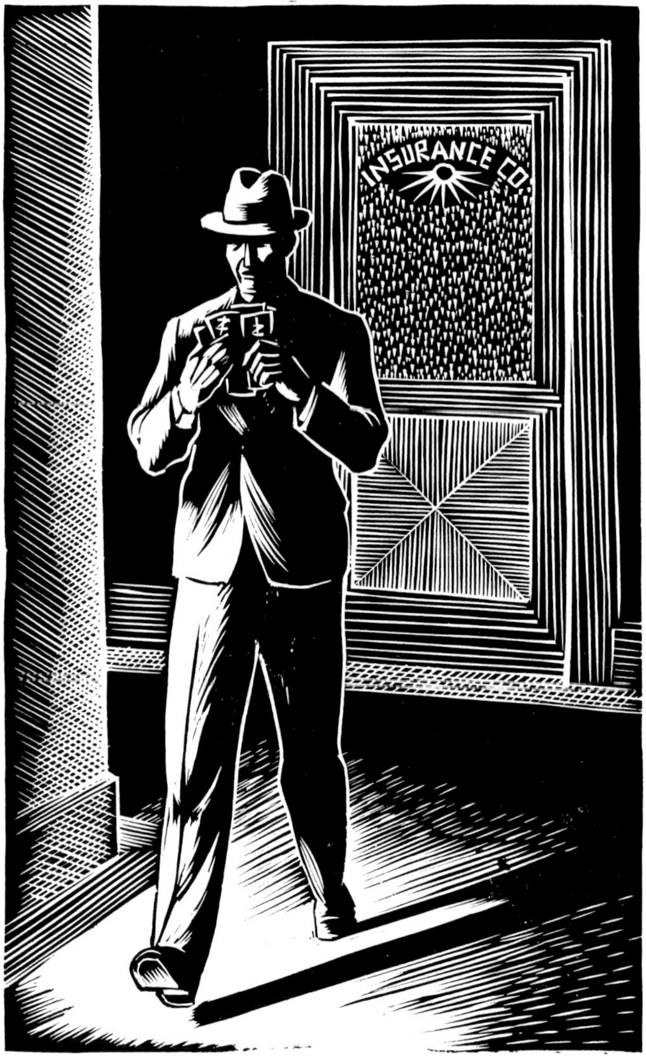
INSURANCE CO.

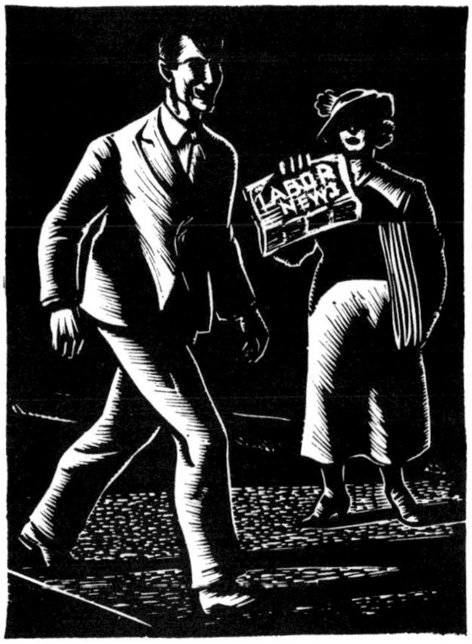
LABOR
NEWS

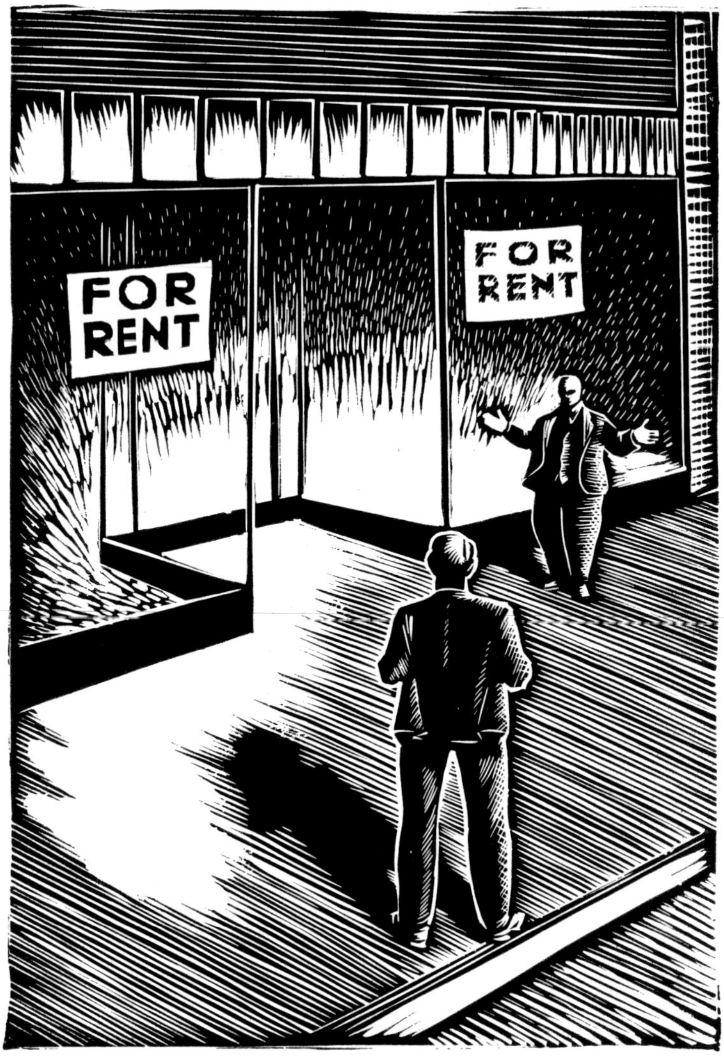
FOR RENT
FOR RENT

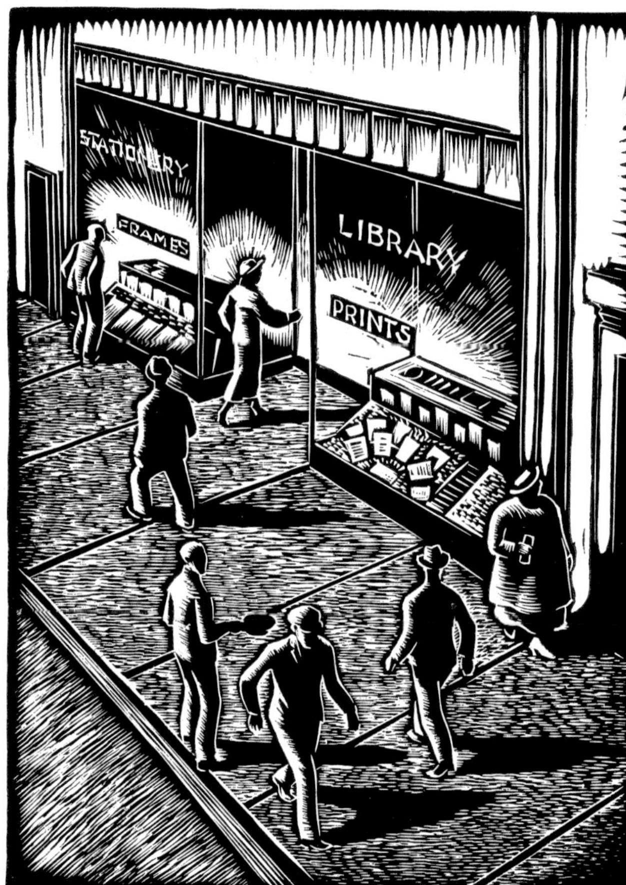
STATIONERY
FRAMES
LIBRARY
PRINTS

CHA N ST RE IN

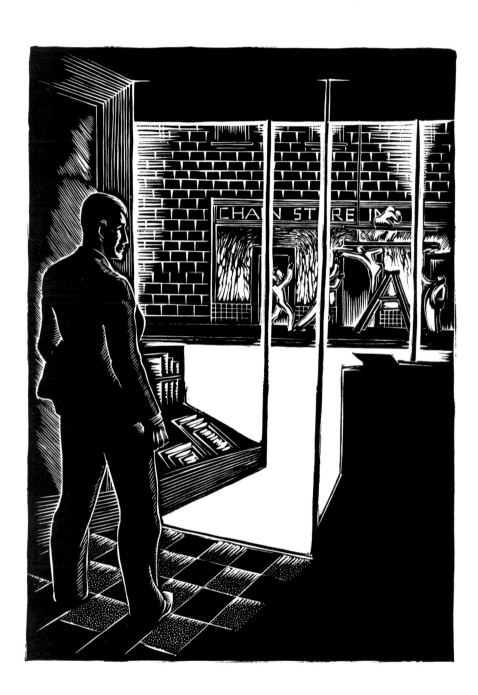

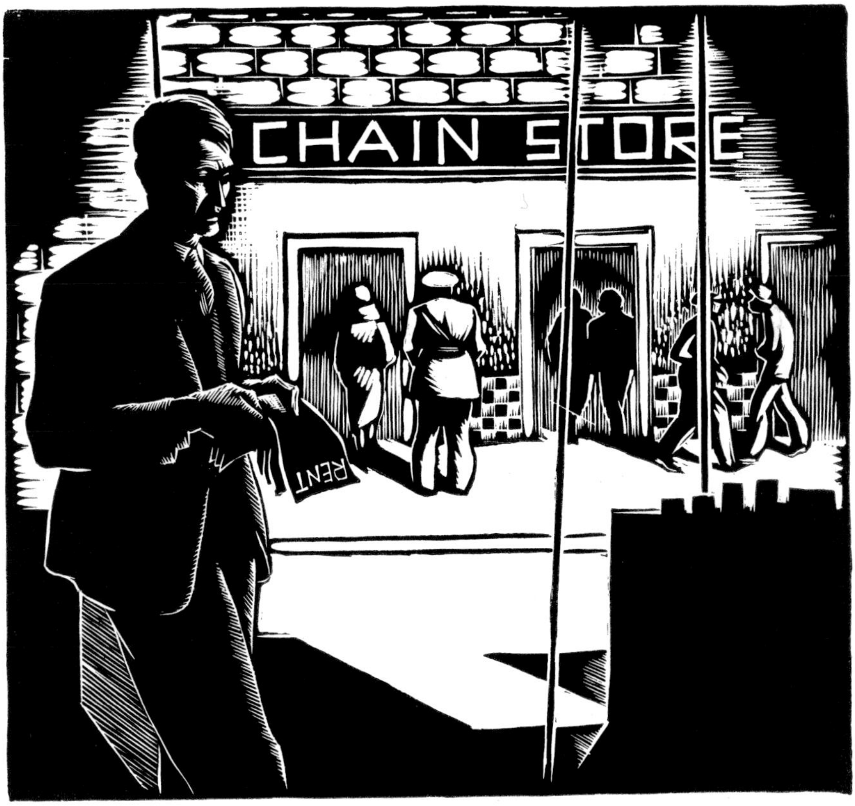
CHAIN STORE
RENT

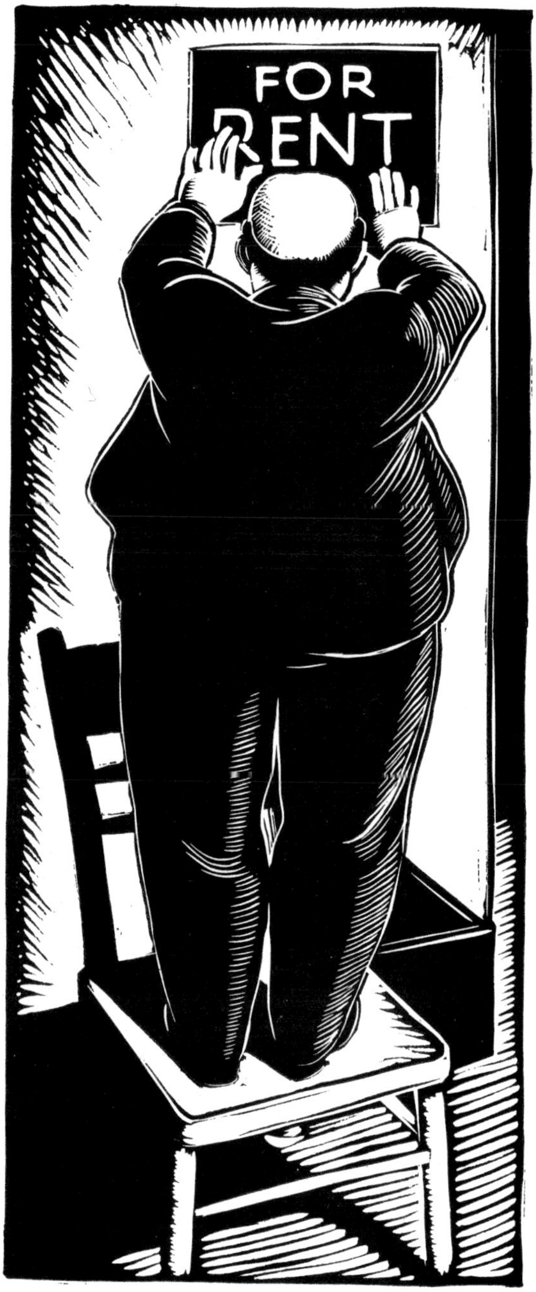
FOR
RENT

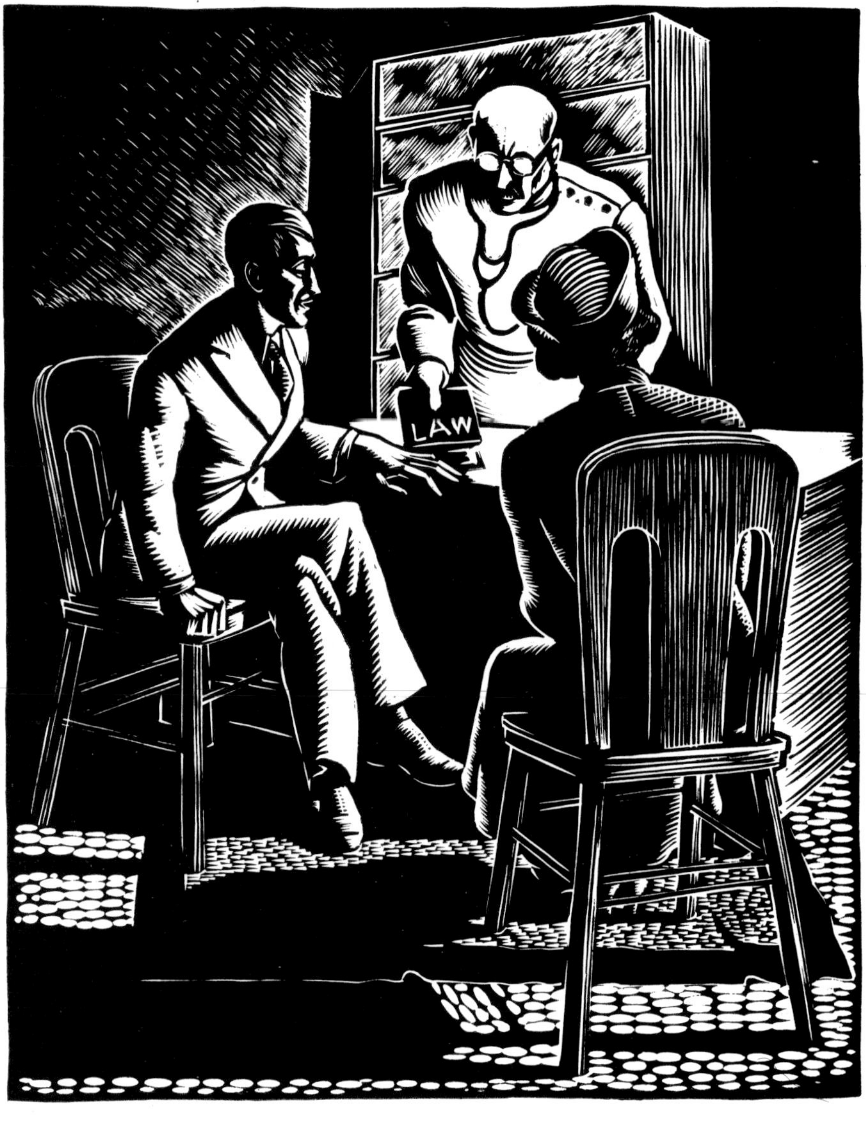
LAW

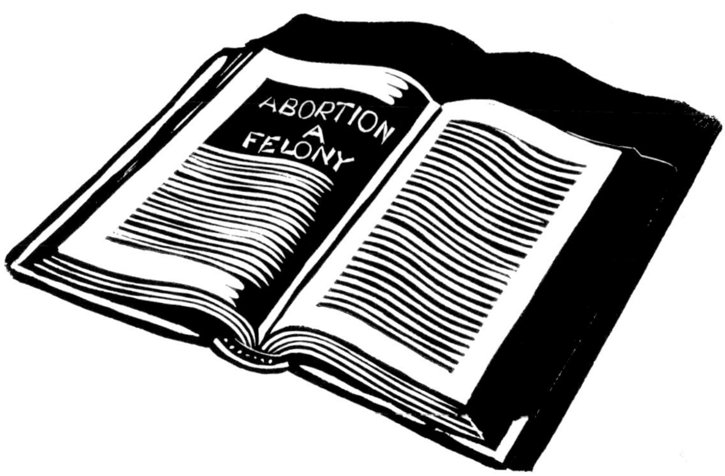
ABORTION
A
FELONY

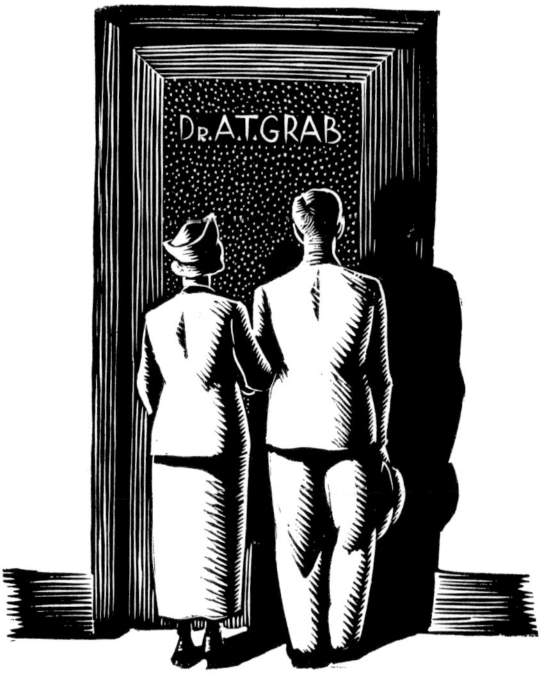
Dr. A.T. GRAB

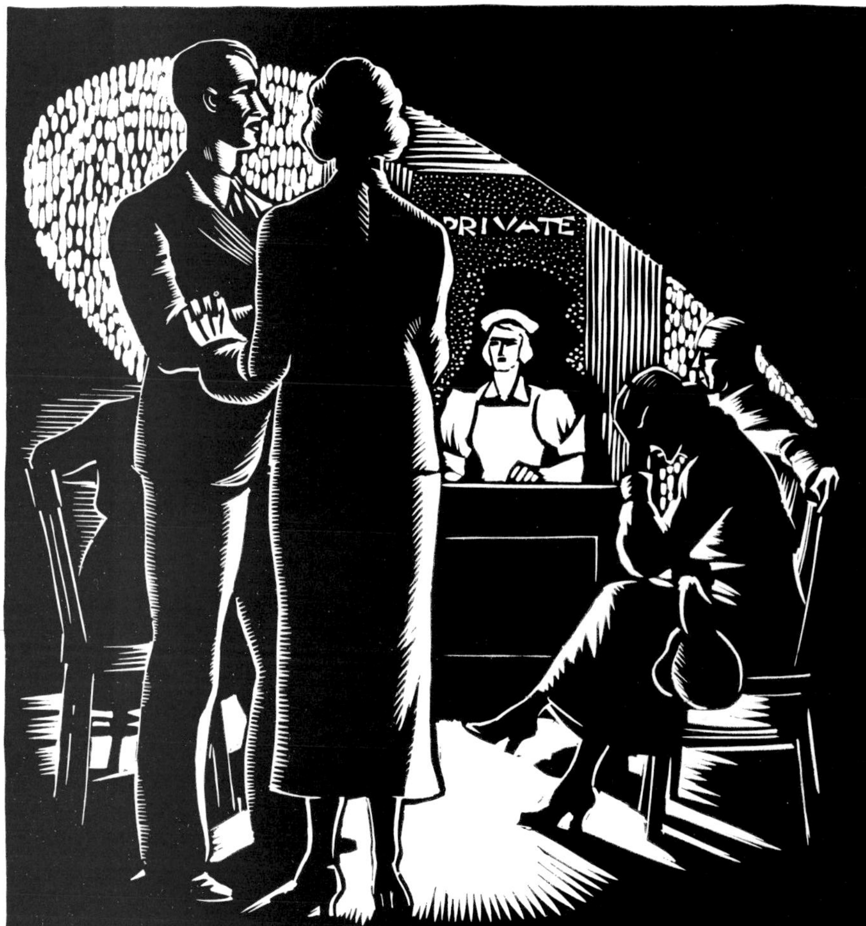
PRIVATE

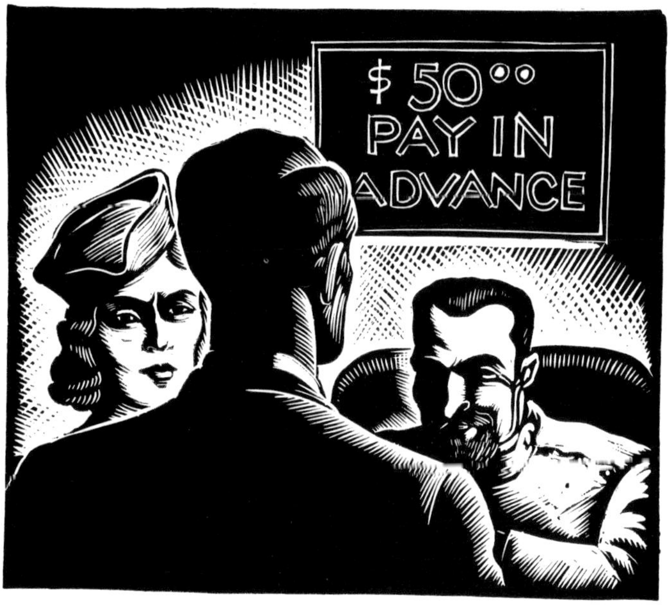
$ 50°°
PAY IN
ADVANCE

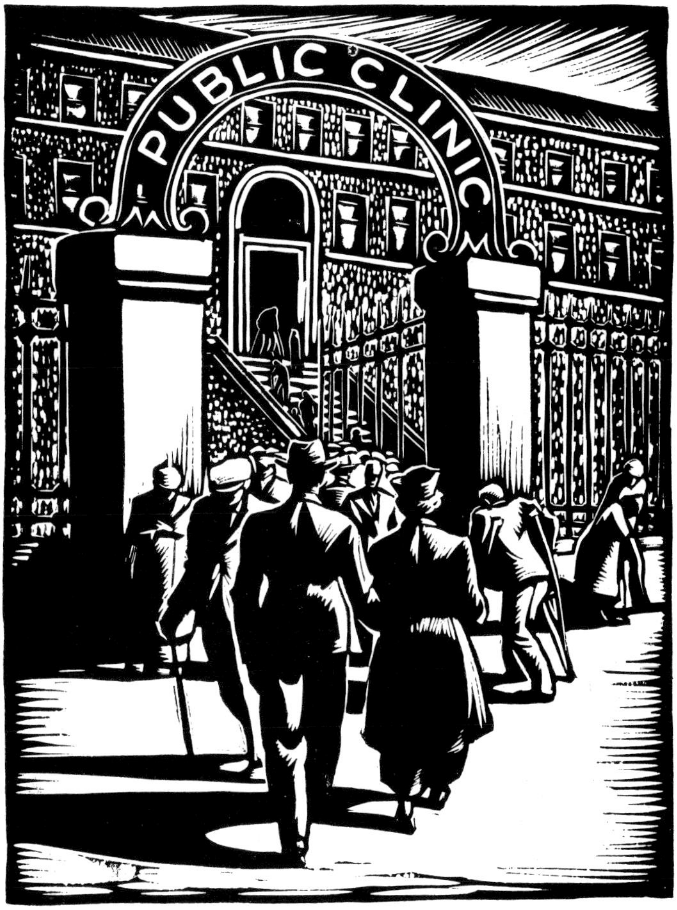
PUBLIC CLINIC

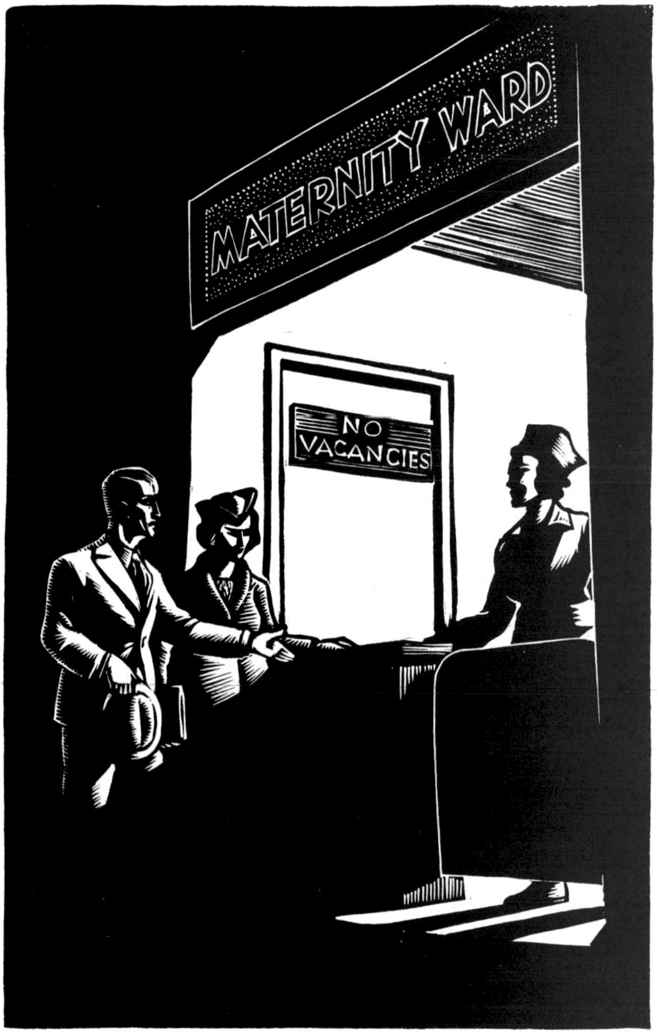
MATERNITY WARD
NO VACANCIES

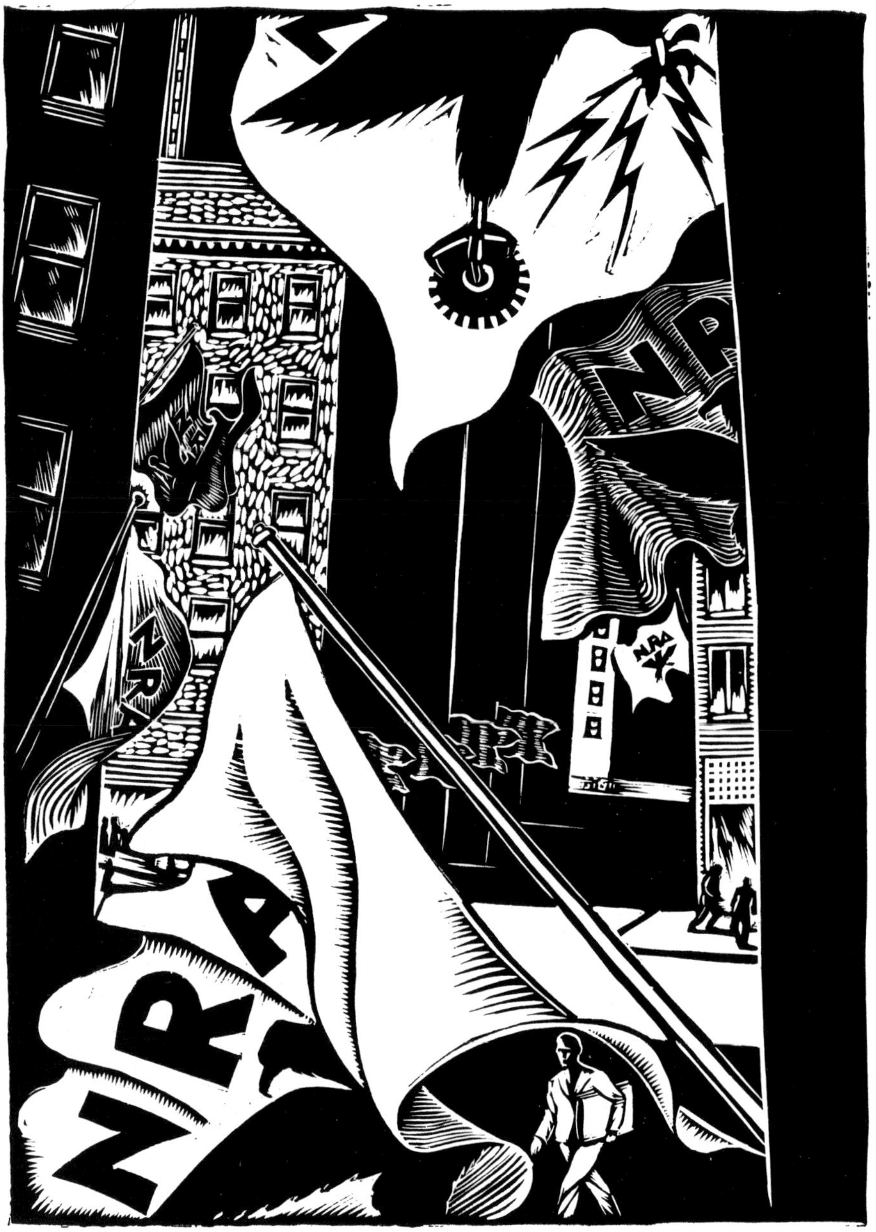
NRA
NRA
NRA

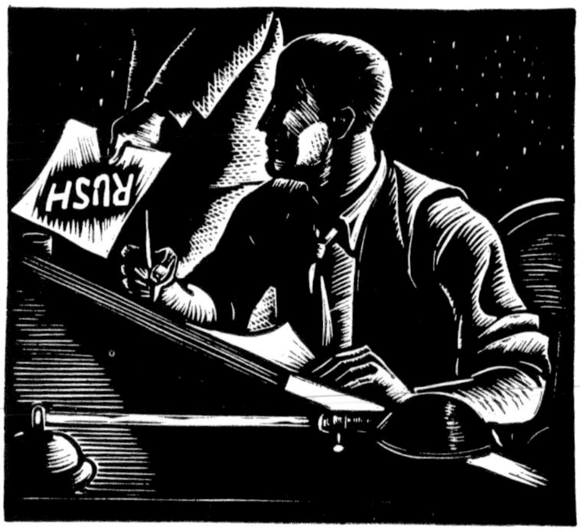
RUSH

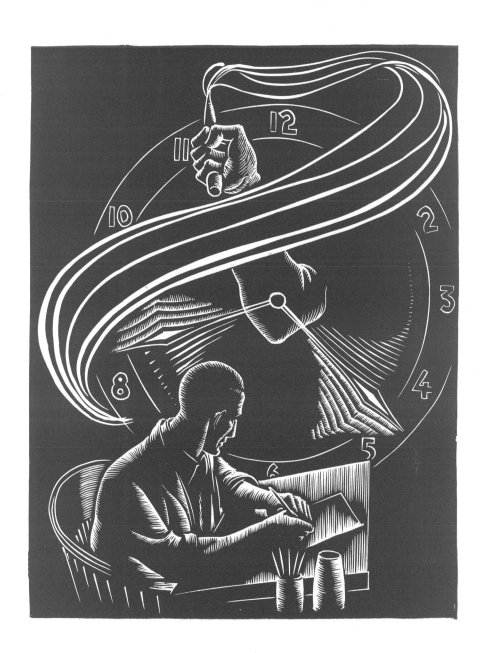

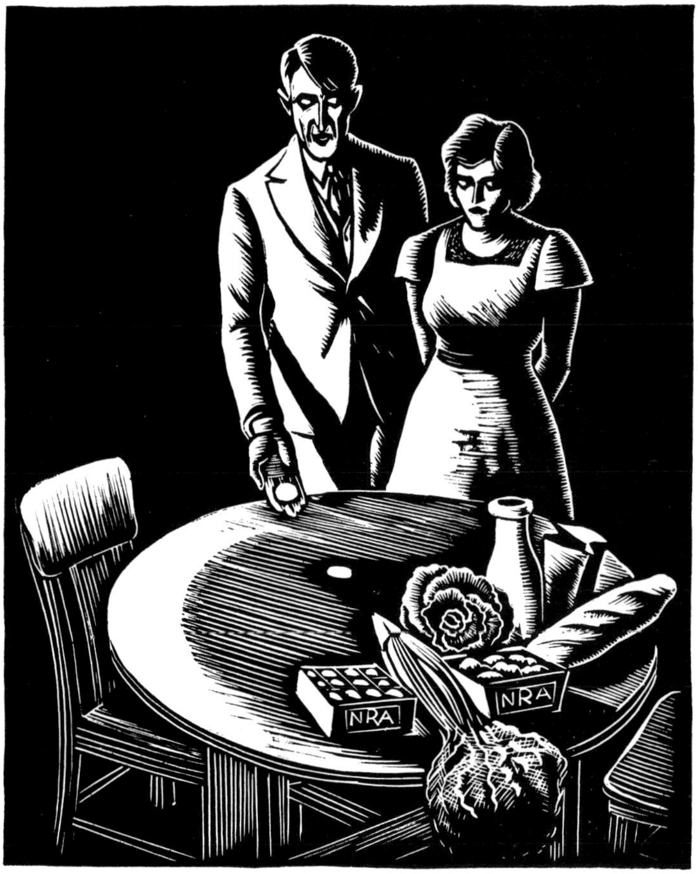
NRA
NRA

GIACOMO PATRI

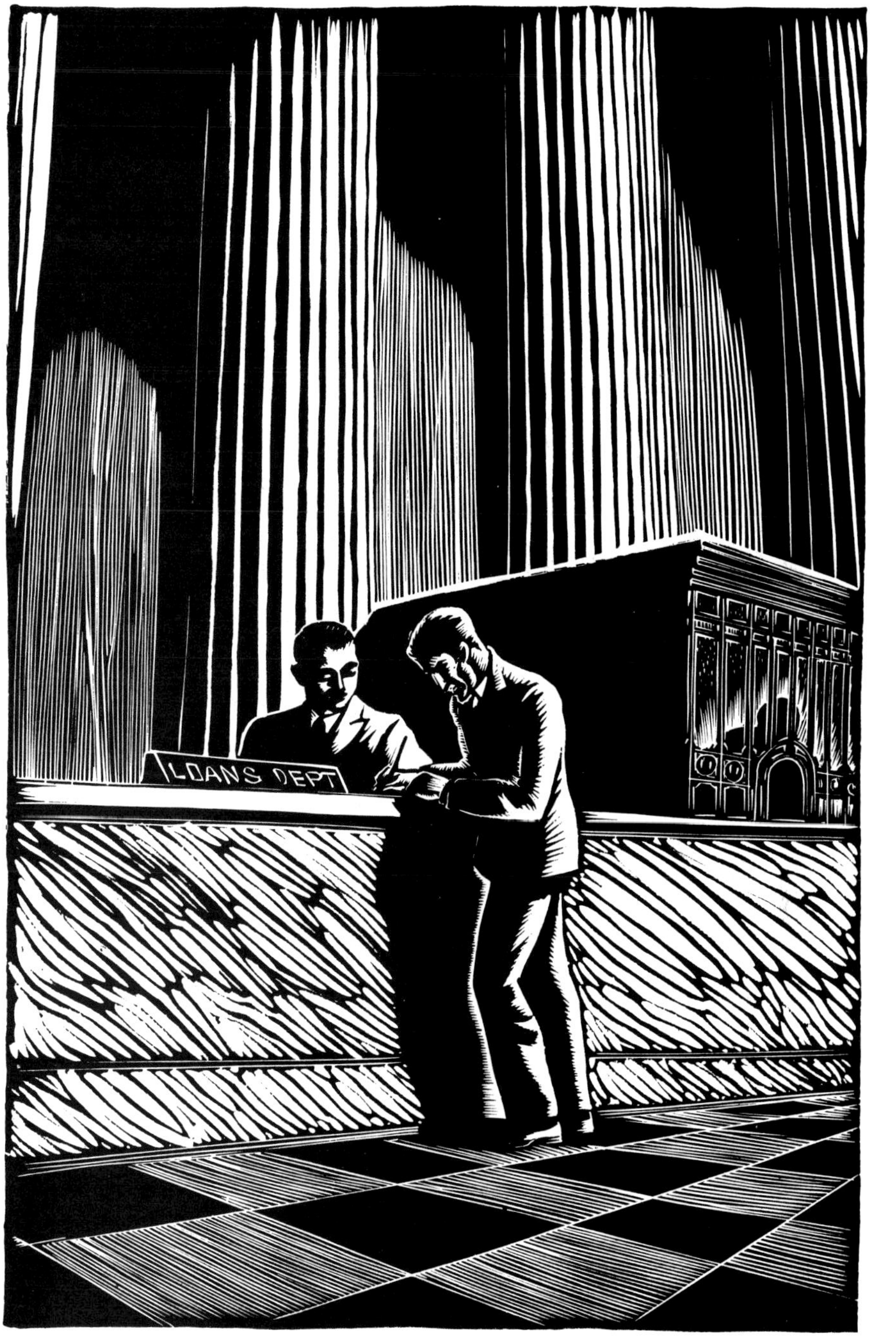
LOANS DEPT

GIACOMO PATRI

RECEIVED

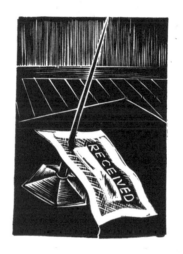

RECEIVED

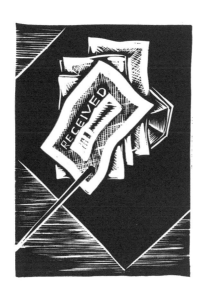

GIACOMO PATRI

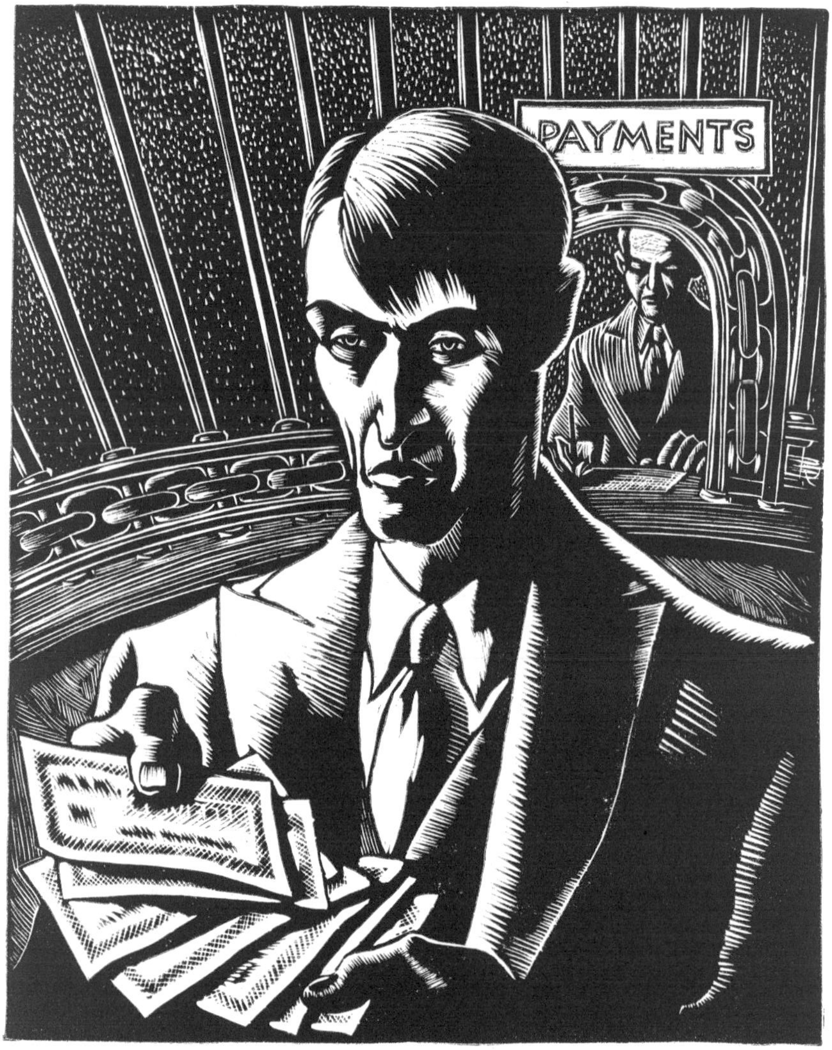
PAYMENTS

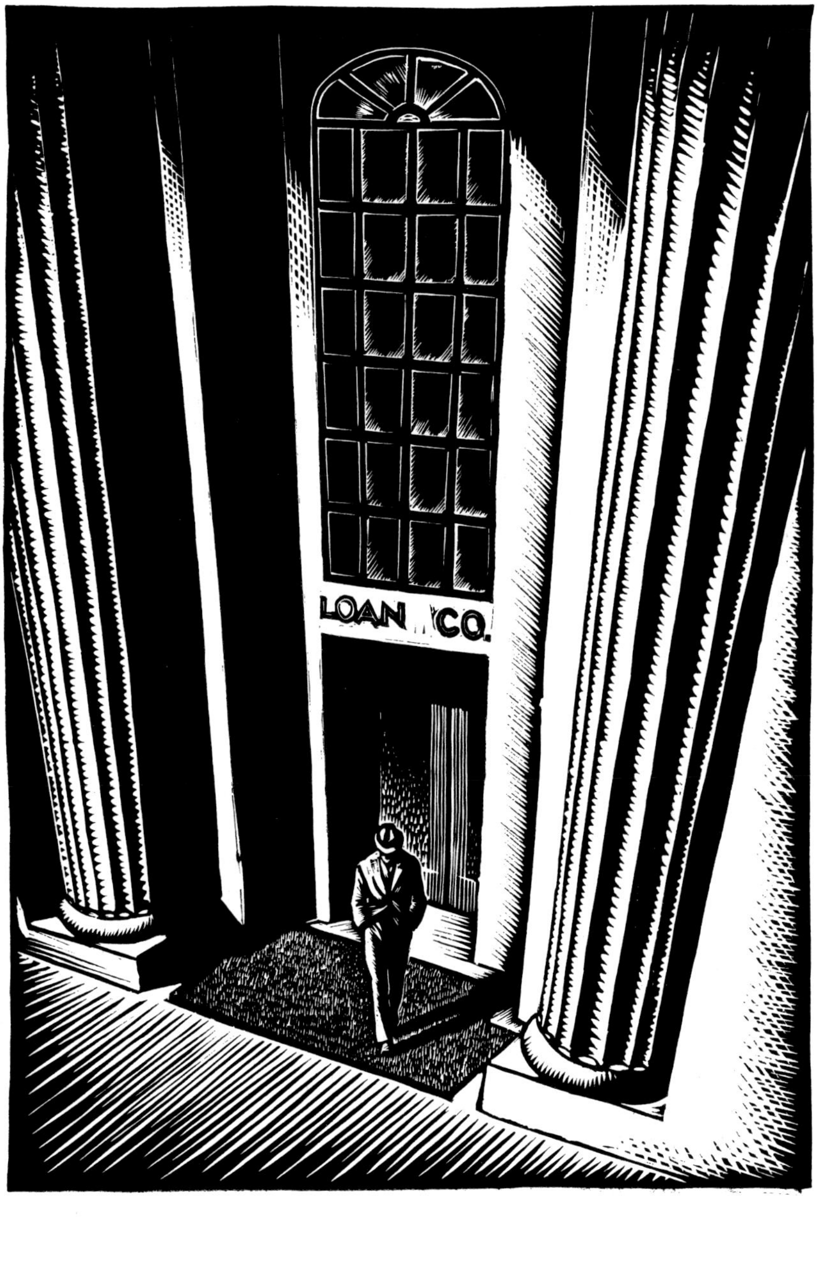
LOAN CO.

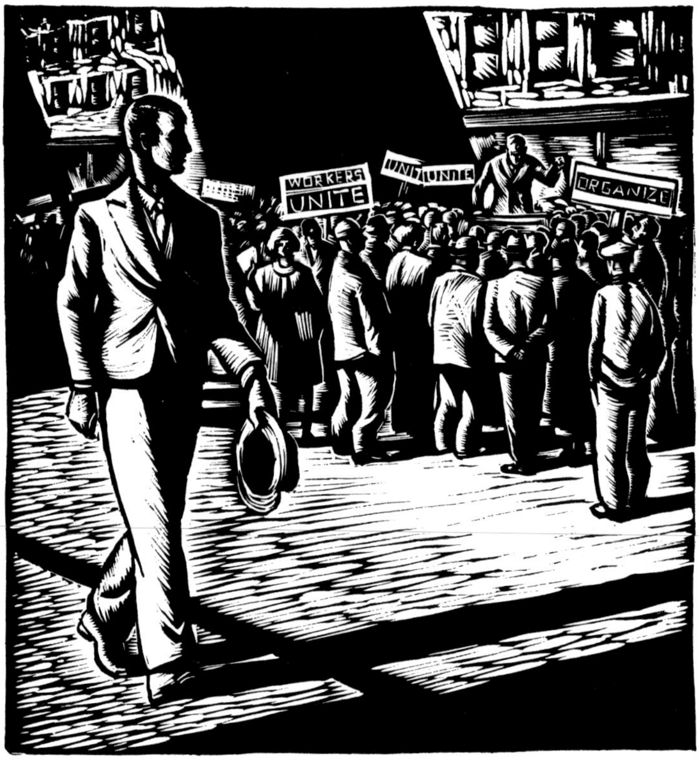
WORKERS UNITE
UNITE
ORGANIZE

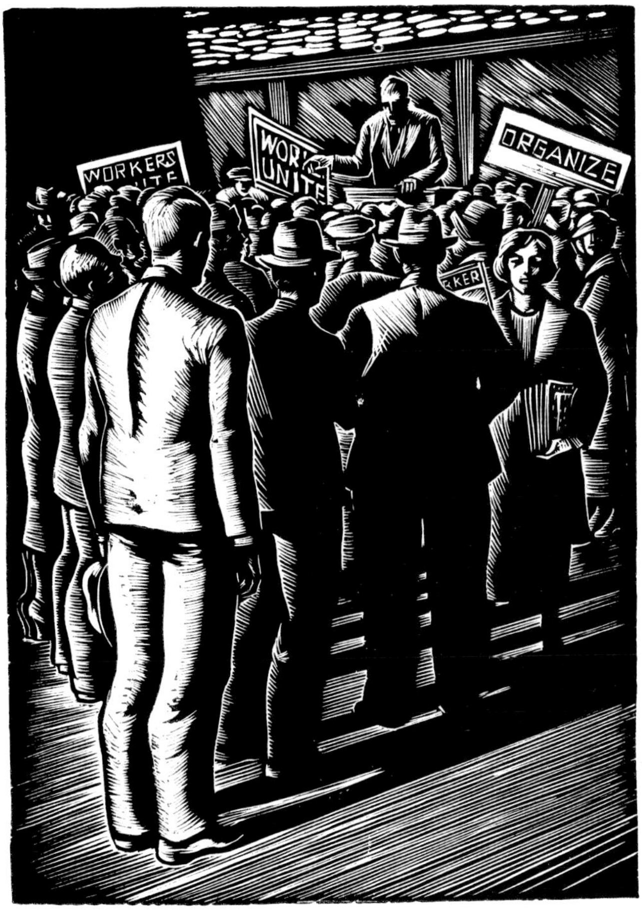
WORKERS
WORK
UNITE
ORGANIZE

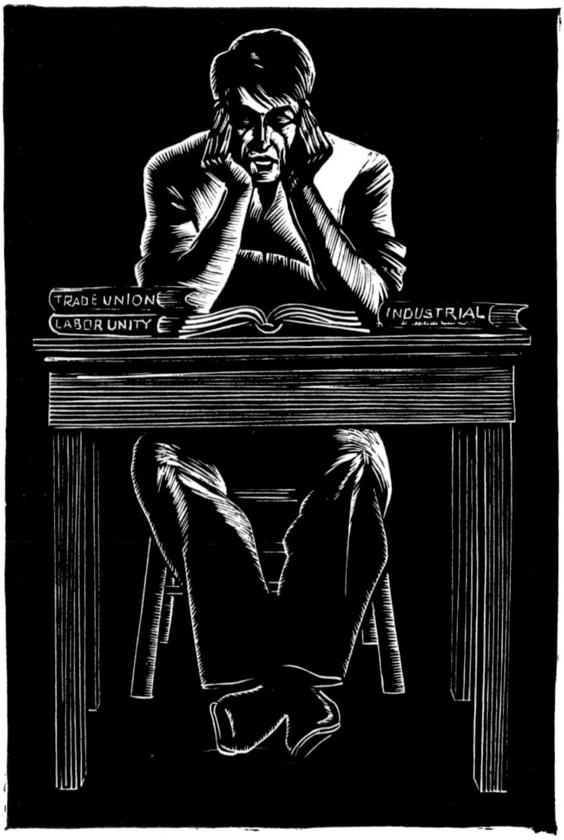
TRADE UNION
LABOR UNITY
INDUSTRIAL

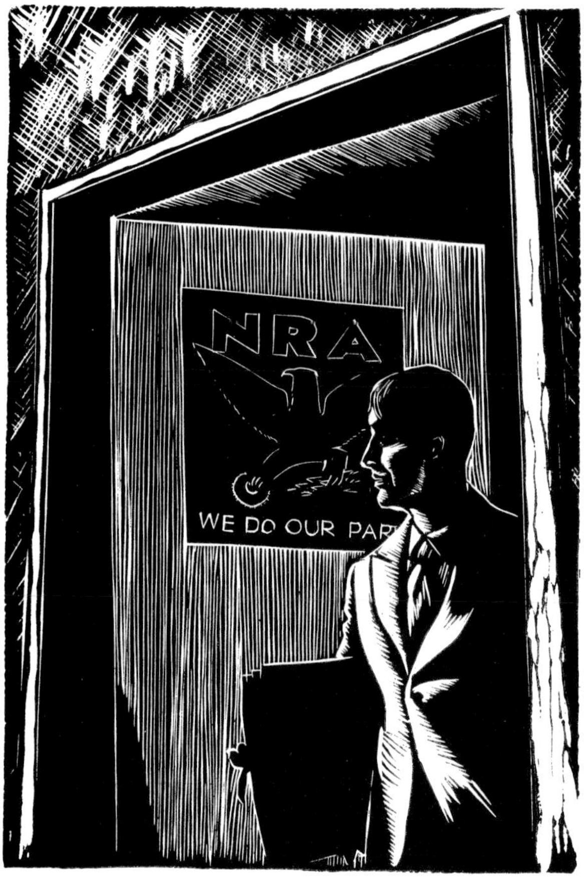
NRA
WE DO OUR PAR

GIACOMO PATRI

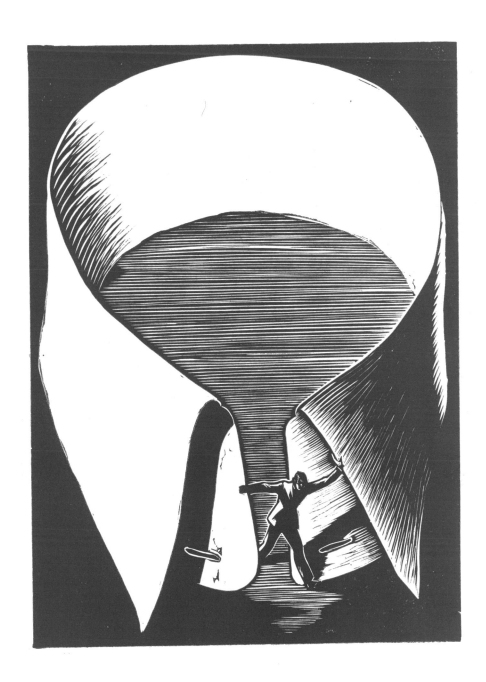

GIACOMO PATRI

LAURENCE HYDE

SOUTHERN CROSS

SOUTHERN CROSS

A Novel of the South Seas

Told in Wood Engravings by LAURENCE HYDE

LAURENCE HYDE

LAURENCE HYDE

LAURENCE HYDE

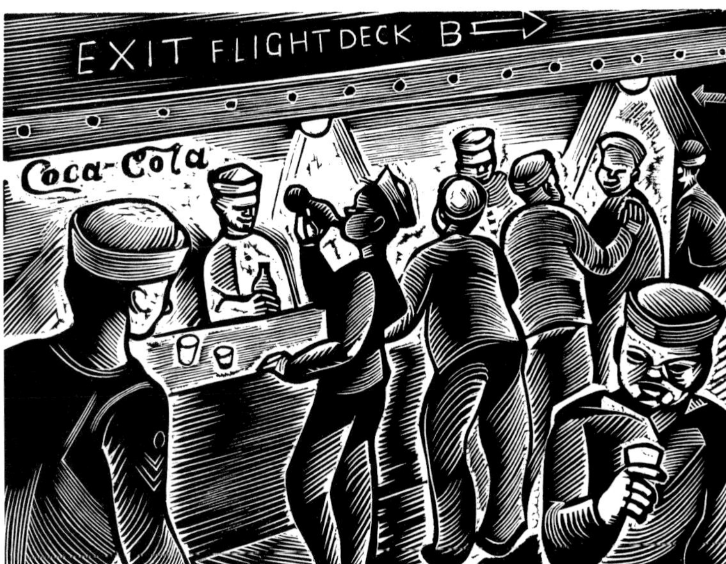
EXIT FLIGHT DECK B
Coca-Cola

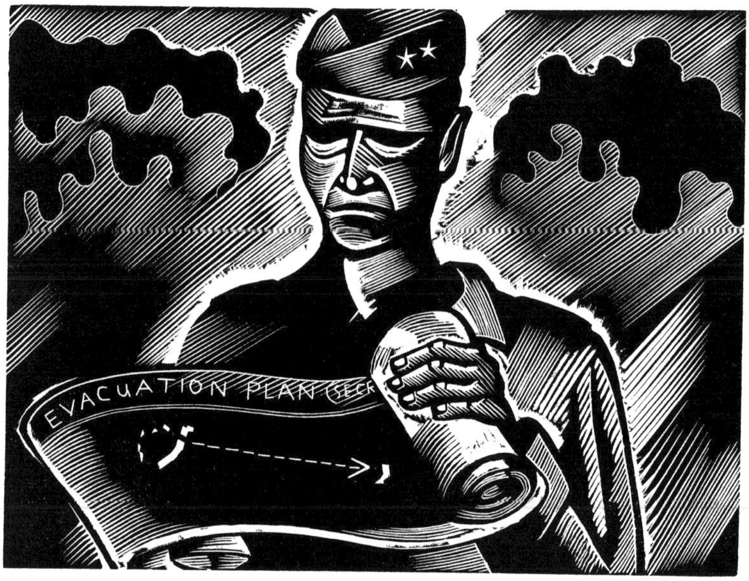
EVACUATION PLAN

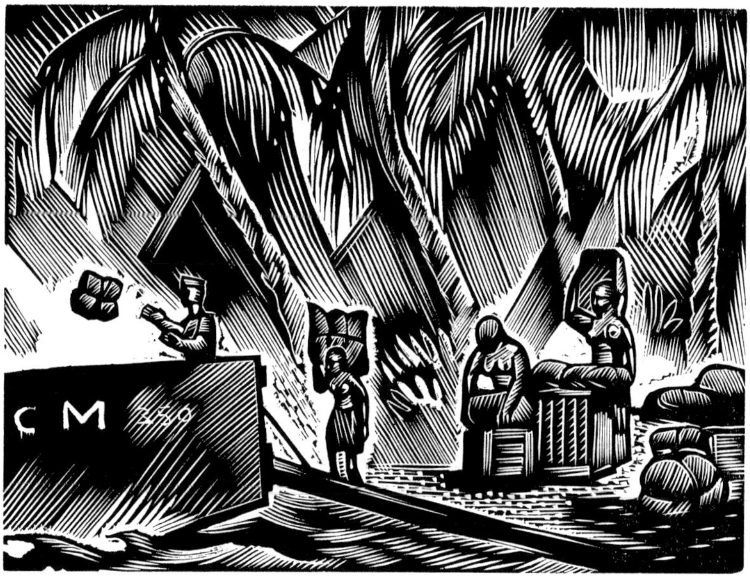
CM

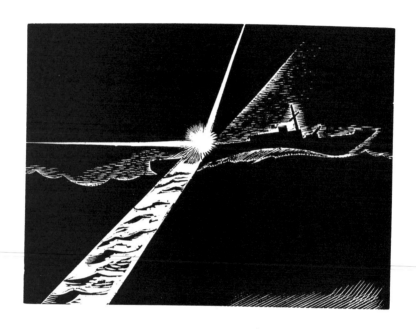

LAURENCE HYDE

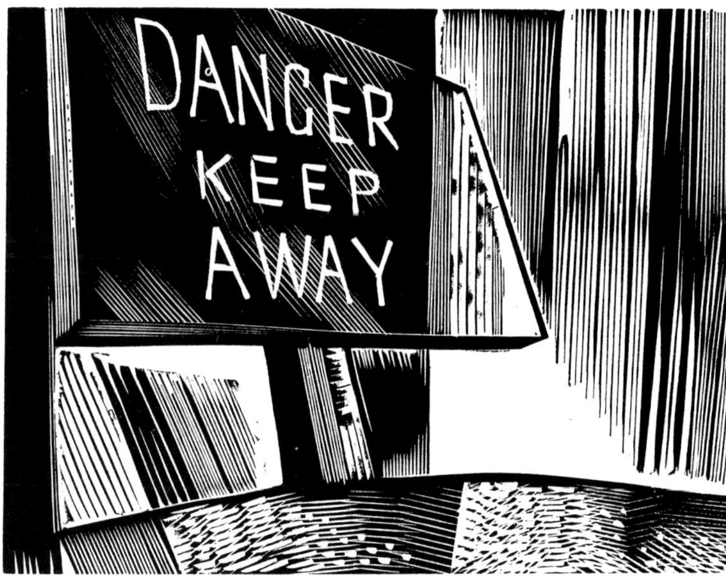
DANGER
KEEP
AWAY

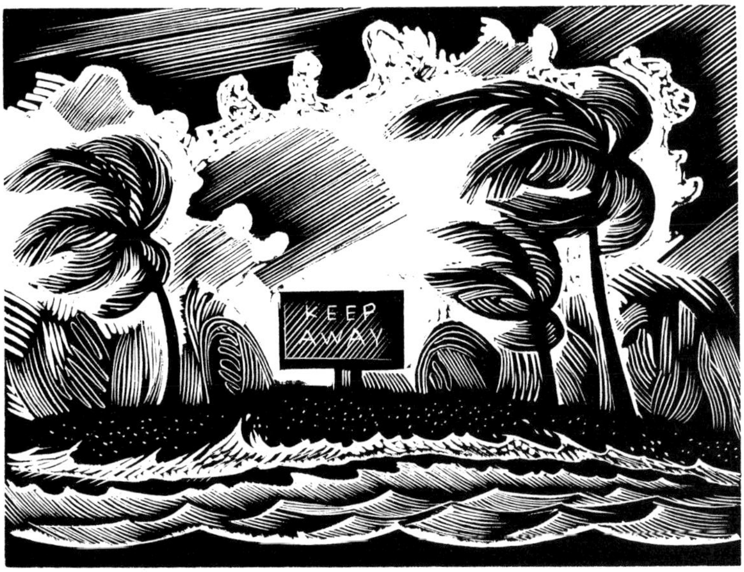
KEEP
AWAY

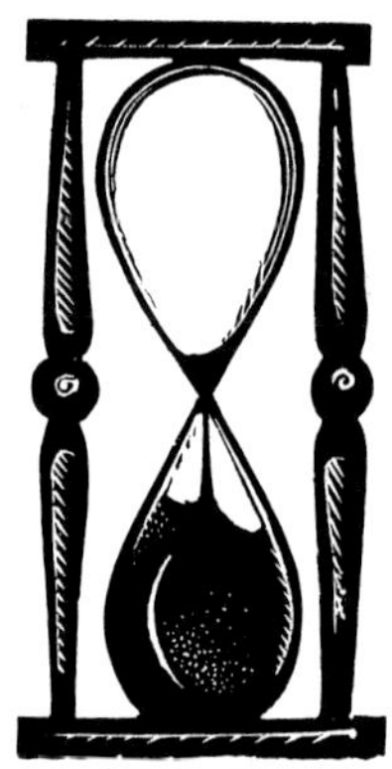

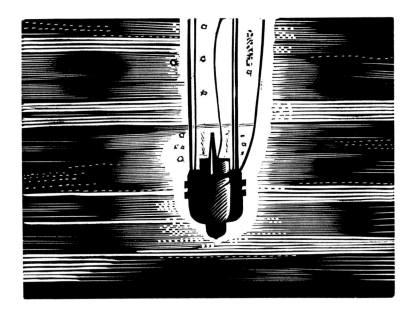

LAURENCE HYDE

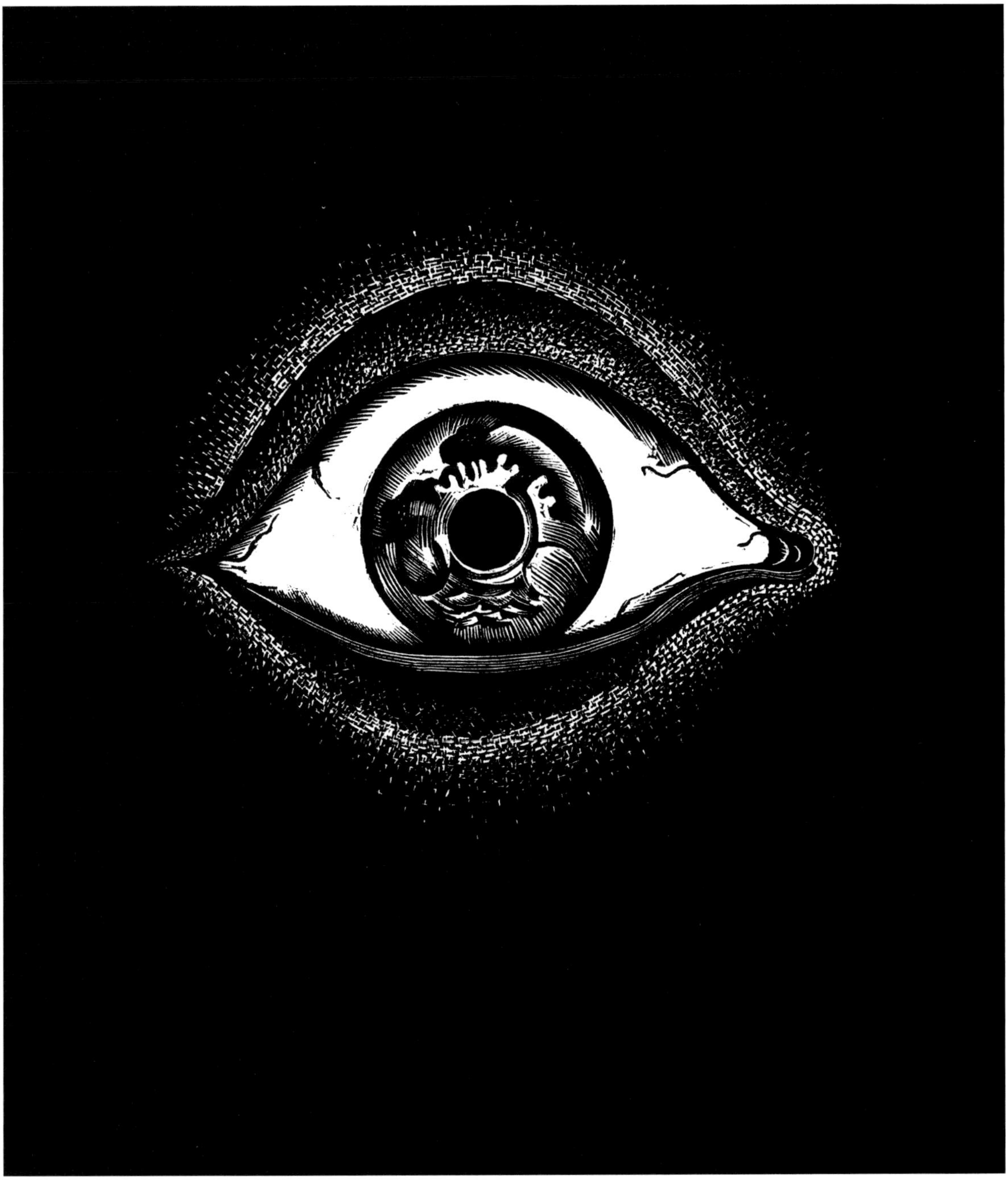

AFTERWORD

I first laid eyes on one of these wordless woodcut novels back in the 1980s when I was just a young pup of a cartoonist and still very wet behind the ears when it came to the history of my own medium. An older, more knowledgeable cartoonist had pulled a copy of Lynd Ward's *Madman's Drum* off his bookshelf and pronounced that it was an early and serious attempt at a comics novel. At the time, that was an exciting idea to me—a piece of comics history I'd never heard of before. This old book was obviously a work of REAL art—completely free of the pulp fiction origins of modern comics.

Over the next decade I familiarized myself with most of the wordless narrative books of the first half of the 20th century. There were a surprisingly large number of them—at least a dozen come immediately to mind. I was happy to include all these books in my rather fuzzy timeline of the development of the comics novel, but I'm not so sure that Ward, Masereel, Nückel or the others would have been pleased with the idea.

In my personal evolutionary chart that moves from single panel gag-cartoons to the fully realized comics novel, wordless novels sit in there as an important stepping stone between the newsprint adventure comic book of the past and the arty pretensions of today's cartoonists. But this isn't really true. If you look over these wordless novels carefully you'll see that they have almost nothing to do with today's graphic novels except perhaps in one important area—they share the same goal of producing a serious sequential novel for an adult audience.

Sadly, there is no real evolutionary comics chart. Looking back on the various narrative picture-novel attempts before 1975, you quickly realize that a sustained story told in picture form is simply a natural idea. Every few years an artist came up with the concept—either independently, or influenced by similar works—yet each new attempt seemed to sink quickly from public sight, and the idea of a narrative picture novel disappeared until the next such book surfaced. Finally, in the last decades of the 20th century the idea picked up steam, and what we call the graphic novel appears to have somehow gotten a foothold on the bookshelves.

Masereel, Ward and company may have inspired each other for the span of a decade or so, but their influence on other narrative picture novel artists was not lasting. Only a handful of artists followed their lead, including William Gropper, who created the lovely wordless novel *Alay Oop* in 1930 and Milt Gross, the brilliant newspaper strip cartoonist who parodied the wordless novel in his hilariously funny book *He Done Her Wrong*, also from 1930.

Ultimately it's a mistake to see these sublimely crafted wordless novels as mere precursors to today's picture-novels. They stand on their own as fully realized artworks and don't need to be drafted into someone else's history. True, they're undeniably connected to the comics by intent, and I don't wish to lessen them as historical role models, but I suspect that these woodcut novels are more tied to the silent film than they are to the comic strip. The artists who created them would have been entirely familiar with both of these popular and commercial art forms—comics and films would have been hard to avoid at the time. Knowing this, it's not much of a leap to see that the wordless novel boys tried hard to avoid any obvious connection to the one drawn medium that was sequential—the vulgar comic strip. Wordless novels take pains to avoid the two most basic elements of the comic strip—multiple panels and word balloons. They could have used words in their books—nothing was stopping them. But they didn't. Why? The answer must be that they felt that the silent film presented the more potent model.

And who came blame them? In the 1920s, which would you choose as a model to emulate if you wished to produce a serious pictorial novel—the silent film, which created works like *Greed* or *Intolerance*? Or the comic strip, which offered you *Mutt and Jeff* and *Boob McNutt*? The single drawing per page found in these books is, without doubt, more a reflection of the movie screen than the comic book page.

But that doesn't bother me too much. You can't excise them from the history of the graphic novel so easily after all. Whatever their origins and influences, they've still been adopted by modern cartoonists hungry for ancestors. And perhaps, it is the world of today which gets to create its past rather than the other way around. If modern cartoonists choose to see these marvelous books as relatives then that may end up being their spot in history, and that's fine with me. I am happy to adopt these lovely books and their virtuoso authors into my family. They are such vital objects and still have so much to offer—beauty, brutality, empathy, a seriousness of purpose, *joie de vivre*, revolutionary fervor—but most of all, these books reflect the work of artists who fully believed that art can change the world.

I'm gratified to see these four books emerge from the rare book rooms and made accessible once again to a whole new generation. They may just inspire a young woodcut artist to get out his tools or, just as likely, a young cartoonist to pick up his brush.

—*Seth, March 2007*

ACKNOWLEDGMENTS

First I'd like to thank my publishing colleagues: Lionel Koffler, Michael Worek, Barbara Campbell, Dan Liebman, Jacqueline Hope Raynor, Tom Richardson, Kim Sullivan, Jennifer Asling, Trina Milnes and designer Kathe Gray. Thanks also to Seth for his generous contribution and insightful words.

Special thanks to all the families of the artists reproduced in this book. I would like to acknowledge Anthony and Kathy Hyde for the lovely afternoon tea at their home and all the support they have shown for this book and all the information they provided about Laurence Hyde and the making of *Southern Cross*. I am also grateful to Larry McLean for his help. Thanks to Eva Gothein in Germany for the images from Werner Gothein's *The Tightrope Walker and the Clown* and Robin Ward Savage for giving us permission to reproduce Lynd Ward's *Wild Pilgrimage*. I am also grateful to Georges Rey for supplying a copy of *White Collar* and allowing me to read his notes about Giacomo Patri and the California Art scene in the 1930s and 40s.

Thanks to Thomas Dannenberg for his excellent German translations. A special thanks to David Berona for his helpful emails and expert advice on the wordless novel.

Last, but not least, I'd like to extend my thanks to fellow members of the Loving Society of Letterpress Printers and the Binders of Infinite Love, a secret society who are always willing to share their knowledge about the book arts.

BIBLIOGRAPHY

Avermaete, Roger. *Frans Masereel.* New York: Rizzoli International
    Publications, 1977.

Balthus. *Mitsou.* New York: Metropolitan Museum of Art, 1984.

Beronä, David A. "A Pathfinder in Pictures: The Woodcut Novels of
    Lynd Ward," *Antiquarian Book Monthly* 23, no. 10 (1996): 20–23.

———. "Pictorial Narratives: The Woodcut Novels of Lynd Ward,"
    The Comics Journal no. 208 (November 1998): 102–106.

———. "Worth a Thousand Words," *Library Journal* 129, no.4 (2004):
    132.

Bettley, James. *The Art of the Book from Medieval Manuscript to Graphic
    Novel.* London: V & A Publications, 2001.

Bocharakova, Helena. *Childhood,* 1931.

Eisner, Will. *Graphic Storytelling and Visual Narrative.* Tamarac, Fla.:
    Poorhouse Press, 1996.

Engel, Walter. "The World of Frans Masereel," *Tribute: Frans Masereel.
    Art Gallery of Windsor Exhibition Catalogue.* (September 13–
    December 12, 1981): 13–14, 23–24, 35–36, 45–46, 49–52, 59–60,
    73–74, 77–78, 81–82, 85–91.

Gothein, Werner. *Die Seiltänzerin und ihr Clown.* Schwenningen:
    Lovis-Presse, 1949.

Gropper, William. *Alay Oop.* New York: Coward-McCann, 1930.

Gross, Milt. *He Done Her Wrong: The Great American Novel and Not a
    Word In It — No Music, Too.* Garden City, NY: Doubleday, Doran and
    Company, 1930.

Herman, Josef. *The Radical Imagination: Frans Masereel, 1889–1972.*
London & West Nyack, NY: The Journeyman Press, 1980.

Hyde, Laurence. *Southern Cross: A Novel of the Southern Seas.*
Los Angeles: The Ward Ritchie Press, 1951.

Lewen, Si. *The Parade.* New York: H. Bittner, 1957.

Masereel, Frans. *25 Images de la Passion d'un Homme.* Geneva: Éditions
du Sablier, 1918.

———. *Das Werk.* Munich: Kurt Wolff Verlag, 1928.

———. *Debout les Morts.* Geneva: Éditions du Sablier, 1917.

———. *Die Idee.* Munich: Kurt Wolff Verlag, 1928.

———. *Die Passion Eines Menschen.* Munich: Kurt Wolff Verlag, 1924.

———. *Die Sonne.* Munich: Kurt Wolff Verlag, 1926.

———. *Geschichte Ohne Worte.* Munich: Kurt Wolff Verlag, 1927.

———. *Histoire sans Paroles.* Geneva: Éditions du Sablier, 1920.

———. *Landschaften Und Stimmungen.* Munich: Kurt Wolff Verlag, 1929.

———. *Le Soleil.* Geneva: Éditions du Sablier, 1919.

———. *Les Morts Parlent.* Geneva: Éditions du Sablier, 1917.

———. *Mein Studenbuch.* Munich: Kurt Wolff Verlag, 1926.

———. *Mon Livre d'Heures.* Geneva: Éditions du Sablier, 1919.

McCloud, Scott. *Understanding Comics: The Invisible Art.* Northhampton,
Mass.: Kitchen Sink Press, 1993.

Moreau, Clément. [Carl Meffert] *Frühe Arbeiten: 5 Grafikfolgen Limmat
Verlag.* Zurich: Limmat Verlag Genossenschaft, 1983.

Nückel, Otto. *Destiny.* New York: Farrar & Rinehart, 1930.

Patri, Giacomo. *White Collar.* San Francisco: Pisani Printing and
Publishing, 1940.

———. *White Collar.* Millbrae, Calif.: Celestial Arts, 1975.

Reid, James. *Life of Christ in Woodcuts.* New York: Farrar & Rinehart,
1930.

Ward, Lynd. *God's Man.* New York: Jonathan Cape and Harrison Smith,
1929.

———. *Madman's Drum.* New York: Jonathan Cape and Harrison Smith,
1930.

———. *Madman's Drum.* Mineola, NY: Dover Publications, 2005.

———. *Prelude to a Million Years.* New York: Equinox, 1933.

———. *Song Without Words.* New York: Random House, 1936.

———. *Storyteller Without Words.* New York: Abrams, 1974.

———. *Vertigo.* New York: Random House, 1937.

———. *Wild Pilgrimage.* New York: Harrison Smith and Robert Haas,
1932.

NOTES

See Bibliography for full reference information.

p. 16   "politics is a matter of factions…"
Avermaete, 1997. p. 87.

p. 17   "the artist is a witness of his time…"
Avermaete, 1997. p. 84.

p. 25   "he labors under the difficulty…"
Review of *The Life of Christ in Woodcuts* by James Reid, *Time
Magazine,* Monday, Dec. 22, 1930, http://www.time.com/time/
magazine/0,9263,7601301222,00.html?internalid=AC (accessed
December 20, 2006).

p. 25   "It was there that my contact…"
John Skovgaard, "The California Labor School," *Zpub.com,* http://
www.zpub.com/gaw/wordpress/?page_id=17 (accessed Dec 21,
2006).

p. 25   "One day a friend handed me…"
Patri, 1975. p. 3.

p. 29   "In the American experience …"
Ward, 1974. p.125.

INDEX